FREY

God of the World

Ann Gróa Sheffield

Published by Lulu.com

First published 2002.
Second edition 2007.

Portions of the First Edition appeared previously in *The Pomegranate*.

ISBN 978-1-4357-0108-3

All author's royalties from the sale of this work will be donated to Conservation International.

Contents

Acknowledgements

I am indebted to David Carron, Sandra Carron, Joe Mandato, and Bob Stine for proofreading this edition. Lissa Potter's skilful techno-geekery was instrumental in formatting the manuscript for publication. Michael G. Smith provided invaluable help with the cover design. The members of Medoburg Kindred, as always, provided encouragement and support. I am especially grateful to Bob Stine, whose faith in me never wavers. Finally, I honor Yngvi-Frey, whose tale I have done my best to tell, and Sigtyr, whose work I strive to do.

Thank you, one and all. Any errors that remain are, of course, my responsibility.

Preface to the Second Edition

The first edition of this short work on Frey was self-published in the literal sense, and I am forever grateful to Rob Shaver for his efforts with computer and printer, to Bob Stine for his beautiful artwork, and to those early readers who responded to the work with generous enthusiasm. In revising the text for more sophisticated technology, I have taken the opportunity to correct some errors in the earlier edition and also to incorporate some new material. What has not changed is my hope that this book will contribute to greater understanding of Frey and encourage readers to read and consider the original sources about him for themselves.

In transliterating Old Norse words into English, I have generally dropped accent marks and nominative case-endings (e.g. "Frey" for *Freyr*, "Odhin" for *Óðinn*). The character ð is represented by "dh" and þ by "th" in Anglicized words. In quoting from translations, however, I have made no changes to the forms used by the translators. All translations in this work not otherwise attributed are my own. Words denoted by asterisks (e.g. **per*) are forms reconstructed by linguists but not directly attested in surviving texts.

CHAPTER I

The Gifts
of Yngvi-Frey

Open most standard works on Norse mythology, and you will find Frey described as a "fertility god" (e.g., Simek 91; Ellis Davison *Myths* 119). Often, all of the Vanir—the group of gods to which Frey belongs[1]—are lumped together as "fertility figures" (Orchard 173). Unfortunately, this "fertility god" stereotype often leads to a distorted view of Frey[2]. Consider the entries in Table 1 on the next page, which lists terms applied to Frey in the Eddas and sagas. A few are appropriate to a "fertility god," but other titles seem equally apt: War-god. Priest-god. Bright god. High god.

In this work, I seek a more complex understanding of Frey in which his gift of fertility is one among many. An extended quotation from Snorri Sturluson's *Ynglinga saga* will serve to introduce the major themes to be developed. In the early part of the saga, the gods appear but are treated as earthly kings that a credulous populace honored as deities. The first such "king" is Odhin; he is succeeded by Njordh,

---

[1] Frey, his sister Freyja, and their father Njordh are Vanir but are also grouped with the Aesir, to whom Njordh was sent as hostage when peace was made between the two tribes of gods (Snorri *Gylfaginning* 23).

[2] The continuing oversimplification of Frey as a "fertility god" can be attributed in part to the influence of Georges Dumézil. His assignment of Frey to his "Third Function" is discussed in Appendix A.

Table 1. Some terms describing Frey in Norse
literature.

Old Norse	Translation	Source
ágætasti af ásum	most renowned, most glorious among gods	*Gylfaginning** 24
árguð	harvest-god, god of prosperity	*Skáldskaparmál** 14
ása jaðarr	foremost, best of gods	*Lokasenna* 35.4
bani Belja	Beli's bane	*Völuspá* 53.3
Belja dólgr	Beli's foe	*Skáldskaparmál** 14
bjartur	bright	*Völuspá* 53.3
blótgoða	sacrifice-priest	*Sörla þáttur* 1
bróður Freyju	Freyja's brother	*Skáldskaparmál** 14
böðfróðr	battle-wise	*Skáldskaparmál** 14
díar	priest	*Ynglinga saga** 4
fégjafa	wealth-giver	*Skáldskaparmál** 14
folkum stýrir	(one who) guides, governs the people (or, troops)	*Skáldskaparmál** 14
fólkvaldi goða	people's ruler (or, army's leader) of the gods	*Skírnismál* 3.1
fögr álitum	fair, beautiful in appearance	*Gylfaginning** 24
fróði	wise	*Skírnismál* 1.3, 2.3
hofgoðunum	temple-priest	*Ynglinga saga** 5
höfðingi	chieftain, ruler	*Gylfaginning** 37
máttug	mighty	*Gylfaginning** 24
nýtom	providing	*Grímnismál* 43.4

Old Norse	Translation	Source
skírom	shining	*Grímnismál* 43.3
son Njarðar	Njordh's son	*Skáldskaparmál** 14
Vanr, Vanaguð, Vananið	one of the Vanir; Vanir-god; kinsman of Vanir	*Skáldskaparmál** 14
vápnlauss	weaponless, unarmed	*Gylfaginning** 37
veraldargoð	god of the world	*Ynglinga saga** 10
þroska	vigorous, well-developed, manly	*Skírnismál* 38.4

Notes: Page and verse numbers refer to the English translations discussed in Appendix B or listed in the "Works Cited." Norse terms are quoted as they appear in the sources, e.g, *fagr* appears as plural *fögr* because it refers to Frey and Freyja collectively.

*Work by Snorri Sturluson (or poets he cites).

who is followed in turn by his son Frey. The passage below describes Frey's reign (10):

> So Frey took the rule after Niord; he was called *Drott* (or Sovereign) of the Swedes and took scot[3] from them; he had many friends and brought good seasons like his father. Frey built near Upsala a great temple, and set there his chief seat .... In his days began the peace of Frode; then there was also a good season over all the land. The Swedes gave Frey credit for it, and he therefore was much more worshipped than the other gods, as the land folk in his days became richer on account of peace and good seasons than ever before.... Frey then fell sick, and as he neared death, his men took counsel, and let few men come to him; and they built a great howe[4] with a door and three holes in it. And when Frey was dead they bore him in loneliness to the howe, and told the Swedes that he was still alive; they watched him then for three years, and all the scot they hid down in the howe.... The good seasons and peace continued.... When all the Swedes marked that Frey was dead, but that good seasons and peace still continued, they believed that it would be so, so long as Frey was in Sweden; therefore, they would not burn him, but called him god of the earth, and ever after sacrificed to him, most of all for good seasons and peace[5].

Snorri's account has several interesting features. First, there is the emphasis on "good seasons and peace." The word *ár*, which Monsen and Smith translate as "good seasons," appears six times in the Old Norse text of this brief

---

[3] "Scot" is a type of tax (the word survives in the term "scot-free").
[4] "Howe" = burial mound.
[5] Translation by Monsen and Smith (Snorri *Heimskringla* 7-8).

chapter; *friðr* (translated "peace" in the quoted passage) occurs five times. Snorri repeatedly associates the same terms—*ár* and *friðr*—with Frey in his works. In *Gylfaginning*, he writes that "it is good to pray to [Frey] for prosperity [*árs*] and peace[6] [*friðar*]" (24). In *Hákonar saga Aðalsteinsfóstra*, toasts are drunk to Odhin for victory, but to "Niord and Frey for good seasons [*árs*] and peace[7] [*friðar*]" (14). Finally, *ár* and *friðr* are mentioned again and again in *Ynglinga saga* in descriptions of the reigns of successful kings. This leads to the next key point about Frey—he is the founder of the Yngling royal dynasty that ruled Sweden for generations (*Heimskringla Prologus*; *Ynglinga saga* 10). The blessings brought by Frey are associated both with living kings and with ancestral kings in the grave-mound. Snorri reports that Frey himself introduced the custom of mound-burial, which replaced the earlier practice of cremation (*Heimskringla Prologus*). Archaeological evidence shows that burial and cremation were in fact practiced contemporaneously (Ellis), so Snorri's account records a myth rather than a historical fact, but the association of Frey with mound-burial is nonetheless significant. Ellis has summarized the literary evidence for sacrifice to kings' burial mounds in Heathen Scandinavia, and her findings confirm that the "dead" king/god in the mound was seen as an active presence—he received sacrifice, and cared for his people in return.

In this work, each of these ideas—divine kingship, *ár*, and *friðr*—will be examined in detail. An additional chapter will tackle the difficult question of Frey and sexuality—difficult, because sex had a peculiar horror for the Christian clerics who recorded most of the evidence, so the

---

[6] Faulkes' translation (Snorri *Edda* 24).
[7] Translation by Monsen and Smith (Snorri *Heimskringla* 87).

sources are few and hard to interpret. Finally, I will bring these ideas together and present my conclusions about Frey.

CHAPTER II

Sacred King, Divine Ancestor

The connection between Frey and kingship is clearest in Sweden, where Frey was the ancestor of the royal Yngling dynasty[1]. Frey is called *blótguð Svía*, "sacrifice-god of the Swedes," in *Ögmundar þáttur dytts*. Place-names such as *Freysakr* ("Frey's field") and *Freyslundr* ("Frey's grove") are much more common in Sweden than anywhere else in Scandinavia (Turville-Petre 168). In *Hallfreðar saga vandræðaskálds*, a group of seamen promises "a large sum of money to Frey if they got a wind to Sweden, or to Thor or Odin if they reached Iceland[2]" (233).

The Yngling royal house that descended from Frey took its name from the god, who is frequently called Yngvi-Frey, Ingunar Frey, and the like in Norse literature. Snorri states directly, "Frey was known by a second name Yngvi[3]" (*Ynglinga s.* 10). The etymology of Yngvi/Ing is obscure, but Snorri does cite a skaldic verse by Markus that uses *Yngvi* as

---

[1] After many generations, the evil Yngling king Ingjald the Ill-minded was killed and his son Olaf fled to Norway; his descendants included many of Norway's greatest kings (Snorri *Ynglinga s.* 41-50, *Hálfdanar s. svarta* 6-7). Despite the eventual removal of the Yngling line to Norway, however, Frey's close relationship with Sweden remained strong.

[2] Whaley's translation ("The Saga of Hallfred the Troublesome Poet" 233).

[3] Translation by Monsen and Smith (*Heimskringla* 7).

a term for "king" (*Skáldskaparmál* 80). A group called the Ingvaeones is mentioned by the Roman writer Tacitus (77). Rives concludes that the tribal name is authentically Germanic (109-11) and summarizes the argument that it means "those belonging to [the god] **Ingwaz* (113), i.e., to Ing/Yngvi[4].

The meaning of "Frey" is better understood: the word is not properly a name but rather a title meaning "lord." It descends from Proto-IndoEuropean **per* ("forward, through"). This early sense was expanded to include meanings such as "chief, foremost," which led to Proto-Germanic **frawan*, "lord" (Watkins 65). The term survives in Old Norse only in the deity-names Frey and Freyja, but several cognates exist in other Germanic languages. Green examines these cognates in detail and concludes that the term originally denoted the head of an extended household but became associated with gods as well as human rulers at a very early (pre-Christian) date in Germanic culture. He further notes that the Old High German adjective *frôno* can mean "to do with a lord or lords" or "public, communal[5]" but also "belonging to the gods, holy." He stresses that, because *frôno* derives "from a genitive *plural* suitable for the needs of a polytheistic religion" (emphasis in original), the meaning "holy" must antedate Christianity (102-6). Yngvi-Frey is thus "Lord Yngvi" or "the holy god Yngvi."

Snorri's *Ynglinga saga* recounts the lives of the Yngling kings descended from Frey. Like the god, most have reigns characterized by peace and prosperity. A notable exception is King Domaldi, whose fate shows the vital importance of the

---

[4]**Ingwaz* is also the reconstructed name of the 22nd rune in the Elder Futhark. The Anglo-Saxon *Ing*-rune and its connection with Frey will be discussed below

[5]Green suggests that the sense "public, communal" for *frôno* derives from the fact that the assembly responsible for law and justice was composed of eminent men in the community who "deliberate as a body" and constitute "public authority" (103).

king to the land. A dire famine occurs during his reign. The first year, the people sacrificed oxen to no avail. The second year, they sacrificed men, but the crops failed again. The third year (15):

[M]any Swedes came to Upsala at the time when the sacrifice [*blót*] should be held. The chiefs then took counsel, and held to a man that Domaldi their king must be the cause of the bad seasons and also that they should have to sacrifice [*blóta*] him in order to have a good season [*árs*], that they should bear their weapons against him and kill him and dye the altars with his blood. And so they did[6].

The ill-fated king was succeeded by his son Domar, and once again "there were good seasons and peace[7]" (16). A similar fate befalls Olaf Tree-feller, a Yngling scion who took refuge in Norway. A large number of Swedes joins him there, but when the crowding leads to a shortage of food, they burn Olaf as a sacrifice because "the Swedes were wont to give the king the blame for both good and bad years[8]" (43).

In Denmark, the blessings associated with Frey are connected to "King Frodhi." The traditions surrounding this king, or rather kings, are difficult to sort out. Several historical and semi-historical characters bore the name. Saxo Grammaticus describes a number of them, and Ellis Davidson ("Introduction" I.114; "Commentary" II.72) notes that Saxo has conflated the stories of *Frið-Fróði* ("Peace-Frodhi") and *Fróði inn fræknae* ("Frodhi the Bold"). The former is important here: Snorri reports that, during Frey's reign in Uppsala, the *Fróðafriðr* ("Frodhi's *friðr*") held sway (*Ynglinga s.* 10) and that the *Fróðafriðr* was remembered in

---

[6] Translation by Monsen and Smith (Snorri *Heimskringla* 10-11).
[7] Translation by Monsen and Smith (11).
[8] Translation by Monsen and Smith (32).

the North as a legendary time when *friðr* was known all over the world (*Skáldskaparmál* 52). Another myth associated with *Frið-Fróði* is that of Frodhi's mill, which ground out wealth and peace for the king. This myth is the subject of the Eddic poem *Gróttasöngr* and will be discussed in Chapters III and IV below. A final connection between the king and the god is the name "Frodhi" itself. The word literally means "learned, wise," and, in the Eddic poem *Skírnismál*, Frey himself is called *enn fróði*, "the wise" (1.3, 2.3). Among men, the same phrase is applied only to those renowned for their learning such as Ari Thorgilsson and the Venerable Bede[9].

Saxo's account of King Frodhi's death (I.157-8) bears a striking resemblance to Snorri's description, quoted in Chapter I, of the death of Frey:

> [The] nobles kept [Frodhi] embalmed for three years, since they feared the provinces would revolt if their sovereign's end became known. They particularly wanted to keep his death concealed from outsiders, so that they could protect what had long been the far-flung bounds of his empire, and with the support of their leader's old power draw the customary tribute from their subjects. For this reason, they would draw his lifeless body about, not, so it seemed, in a hearse, but a royal carriage[10][.]

---

[9] Some scholars (e.g., Dronke 404-5, Turville-Petre 170) prefer to translate the occurrence of *fróðr* in *Skírnismál* as "fruitful," but I am not convinced by the argument for doing so and suspect it derives from a presupposition that anything to do with Frey must necessarily be connected to fertility. Cleasby and Vigfusson define *fróðr* straightforwardly as "knowing, learned, well-instructed," and no one calls Ari the Learned "Ari the Fruitful."

[10] Fisher's translation.

Saxo also translates into Latin a poem about Frodhi's death that the cleric explains was originally written in "the rude venacular[11]" by Hiarni, who succeeded Frodhi as king of Denmark. Saxo's verse tells how Frodhi's body was carried around the countryside for a time but now lies in the earth (I.162). If, as Saxo claims, his verse is based on a Danish original, it suggests that the procession of Frodhi's body is an authentic tradition and not just a fantastic invention by the cleric.

Additional parallels exist between Saxo's account and the description of Frey quoted in Chapter I. The nobles conceal the death of the king for three years but continue to collect scot (tax) or tribute. Like Frey, Frodhi is (eventually) buried rather than burned, and this is an opportune point to consider briefly the evidence for the worship of ancestors and kings who were buried in howes.

The references in Norse literature to veneration of the dead in general, and of the grave-mound in particular, has been summarized by Ellis in her invaluable work *The Road to Hel*. Apart from Snorri's account about Frey himself, the clearest example of sacrifice to a dead king in the mound is the story of King Olaf Geirstadhaalfr, a descendant of the Yngling line. Before his death, King Olaf instructs his people (*Flateyjarbók* 2: 7):

> There must be no following the example of those who sacrifice [*blóta*] to dead men in whom they put their trust while they were alive[...] I am very much afraid that a famine [*hallære*] will come upon the land after we are laid in howe. And thereupon sacrifices will be made to us, and we will be turned into trolls[12].

---

[11] Fisher's translation.
[12] Translation by Ellis (101).

The authenticity of Olaf's request (recorded by a later, Christian scribe) is suspect, but it is ignored in any case—famine does come upon the land, and the people do sacrifice to Olaf for *ár*. The text implies that, despite the living Olaf's misgivings, the sacrifices to his mound have the desired effect. At this time the people give him the name *Geirstaðaálfr*, the "elf of Geirrstadh."

Elves are elsewhere associated with Frey and with mounds. The Eddic poem *Grímnismál* says that the gods gave *Álfheim*, "elf-world," to Frey as *tannfé*, "tooth-money" (5.3-4); Snorri explains that *Álfheim* is the realm of "light-elves [who] are fairer than the sun to look at[13]" (*Gylfaginning* 17). In *Kormáks saga*, Thorvard is injured by Kormak and asks a wise-woman for advice. She tells him (22):

> There's a certain hillock a short way from here, in which elves [*álfar*] live. You are to take the bull that Kormak killed [after the fight], redden the surface of the hillock with the bull's blood, and make the elves a feast of the meat; then you'll recover.[14]

Other incidents from the sagas reinforce the association of grave-mounds both with Frey and with kings whose prosperous reigns echo the god's. According to Snorri, King Halfdan the Black (a Yngling descendant) was the *ársælstur*, "most *ár*-blessed," of kings, and his body was so much in demand after his death that pieces of it were shared out among four districts. They all raised howes over their alloted relics because "they expected good seasons [*árvænt*] if they had the body[15]" (*Hálfdanar s. svarta* 10). Another king, Holgi, was buried in a howe with "alternately a layer of gold

---

[13] Faulkes' translation (Snorri *Edda* 19).
[14] McTurk's translation ("Kormak's Saga" 217).
[15] Translation by Monsen and Smith (Snorri *Heimskringla* 14).

or silver—this was the money offered in sacrifice [to Holgi]—and a layer of earth and stone[16]" (*Skáldskaparmál* 55). Ellis describes additional examples of sacrifice to howes for *ár*; one such mound is even named *Árhaugr* (104).

Finally, an incident in *Gísla saga Súrssonar* provides a direct link between Frey and the dead buried in mounds. Thorgrim Thorsteinsson was an Icelander noted for his devotion to Frey. After his death, people noticed an odd phenomenon (18):

> Another thing happened that was accounted strange—the snow never settled on the south-west of Thorgrim's burial mound, nor showed any sign of frost. People suggested that Frey had been so endeared by the sacrifices [*blótin*] Thorgrim had made to him that the god had not wanted the ground between them to freeze[17].

To return to Saxo's account: his description of Frodhi's death and the procession of his body around the countryside provides yet another connection—in addition to the association with *ár* and *friðr*, the name "Frodhi," sacrifice to the king/god after his death, and howe-burial—between the mythical king and the god Frey. First, according to Snorri, Frey himself drives a chariot drawn by a boar (*Gylfaginning* 49). Second, a ritual procession involving a chariot is specifically attested for two of the Vanir. Tacitus, a Roman writing in the 1st century C.E. about the Germanic tribes, describes a procession of the goddess Nerthus (93). Nerthus is a feminine variant form of the masculine name Njordh (Simek 230); in later Scandinavian mythology, Njordh is one of the Vanir and Frey's father. Tacitus reports that the visit of the goddess in her chariot was a time of peace and

---

[16] Faulkes' translation (Snorri *Edda* 112).
[17] Regal's translation ("Gisli Sursson's Saga" 21).

rejoicing. Over a thousand years later, a medieval saga-writer described a similar procession for Frey himself in *Ögmundar þáttur dytts*. The story tells of an idol of Frey that is worshipped by the Swedes and served by a beautiful young woman who is considered the god's wife (320). The saga-writer was an unsympathetic Christian who wanted to ridicule the Heathen Swedes, and he describes how Frey is replaced by one Gunnar, who convinces the dull-witted populace that he is the god. Omitting the text that describes this replacement, however, leaves an illuminating account of Heathen belief:

> Now it came to the time that they set out from home, and Frey and his wife were to sit in a cart while their retainers walked in front [...[18]] They went round to feasts throughout the winter [...[19]] But when some time had passed, it became clear that Frey's wife was pregnant. That was taken to be excellent, and the Swedes were now delighted with this god of theirs; the weather too was mild and all the crops so promising that nobody could remember the like[20].

This connection of Frey with wagons occurs again in the Old English *Rune Poem*. As in the excerpt from *Ynglinga saga* quoted in Chapter I, Ing/Frey has been euhemerized and is treated as a mythical hero in the poem. The verse for the rune *Ing* reads[21]:

Ing was first   among the East-Danes

---

[18] The omitted text describes how Gunnar wrestles with Frey, overcomes him, and takes his place in the cart.
[19] The omitted text claims that Gunnar as "Frey" refuses blood sacrifice but cheerfully accepts money and goods.
[20] McKinnell's translation ("The Tale of Ogmund Bash" 320-321).
[21] The original text can be found in Halsall (90).

seen by men, until he afterwards eastward[22]
departed over the wave; the wagon ran after;
thus the hard [men] named the hero.

Two points in this verse are of particular interest. First, the cryptic half-line "the wain ran after" can be interpreted to refer to the Vanic processions described above. Second, the god-king appears and disappears rather mysteriously and goes back "over the wave." The word translated "departed" [*gewát*, from *gewítan*] in the *Rune Poem* has the same dual sense as does "departed" in modern English; *gewítan* means "go, withdraw, go away," but also "die, pass away." This description applies well to another mythical king, Scyld Scefing, whose story is told in the opening lines of *Beowulf*. Scyld is found abandoned in a boat as a child. The boy becomes king of Denmark, founds a dynasty, and has a long and prosperous reign. After his death, his people lay his body in a ship heaped with treasure and send it out across the ocean (43-52):

> Great the wealth his people gave him,
> gifts no worse than once before
> had furnished those who sent him forth,
> alone, an infant, over the waves.
> Then they set a golden standard
> high over head; let the sea have him,
> gave him to ocean; grieved were their spirits,
> mournful their minds. Men know not
> how truly to say— sage in hall or
> hero under sky— who received that cargo.

Scyld's reign, like Frey's and Frodhi's, is remembered as a blessed time for his people. Both Scyld and Frey are the

---

[22] Some editors have suggested emending *ést*, "east" to *eft*, "again, back" (see discussion in Halsall 147).

founders of royal dynasties; in *Beowulf*, Scyld's great-grandson Hrothgar rules a people called synonymously the *Scyldinga* (after Scyld) and the *Ingwina*, "friends of Ing."

In Norse lore, the arrival of Njordh, Frey, and Freyja in Asgardh echoes the mysterious arrivals of Ing and Scyld. In *Ynglinga saga*, Snorri records that, Frey and Njordh come to Asgardh from Vanaheim as part of a hostage exchange after a war between the Aesir and the Vanir (4). Vanaheim is an enigmatic place, and we are told little about it in the surviving sources. The Eddic poem *Vafþrúðnismál* says (39):

> In Vanaheim
> the wise powers shaped him [Njordh]
> and gave him up to the gods as hostage;
> at the end of this age
> he will come back
> home among the wise Vanir.

The verse implies that Vanaheim will survive the final conflagration at Ragnarok; it appears to be a special place set apart from the worlds of men and the Aesir.

Both Frey and Njordh are also associated with ships and their passage "over the waves." Frey has a magic ship called Skidhbladhnir. Made by the dwarves, it is one of the treasures of the gods and is called "best of ships" in *Grímnismál* (43). Njordh's home is called *Nóatún*, "Harbor," and "it is to him one must pray for voyages and fishing[23]" (Snorri *Gylfaginning* 23) Njordh's wife Skadhi complains that the sea-birds at Noatun are so loud she cannot sleep.

In Germanic culture, ships are also connected with death, the journey into ultimate mystery. In 1942, Ellis summarized the archaeological evidence for ship-burial and for related customs such as the representation of ships on Scandinavian memorial stones. At the time she wrote,

---

[23] Faulkes' translation (Snorri *Edda* 23).

literally hundreds of ship-burials dating from 500 C.E. onwards were known in Scandinavia, and new examples continue to be discovered. The literary sources also speak of ship-funerals: Snorri records that the god Baldur was sent on his journey to Hel's realm in his ship Hringhorni, which is launched and set afire (*Gylfaginning* 49). On a more human scale, two prominent saga-age Icelanders noted for their devotion to Frey were given ship-burial. *Vatnsdæla saga* reports that Ingimund the Old was laid to rest in a boat from his ship (23). In *Gísla saga Súrssonar*, when Thorgrim Thorsteinsson[24] died, "[t]hey laid Thorgrim in a boat and raised the mound in accordance with the old ways[25]" (17). The practice of ship-burial unites the idea of a ship and its journey into mystery with the practice of mound-burial and the veneration of buried ancestors who continue to interact with the living.

To summarize: Frey, and kings whose stories suggest that they are identified with or assimilated to the god, are associated with reigns noted for their prosperity and peace. Frey is the divine ancestor whose blessings are brought forth again and again by his worthy successors; he is the benevolent god of the grave-mound who receives sacrifice and grants abundance in return. However, his ultimate origins are wrapped in mystery, and we will return to this numinous quality when we consider his association with the sacred in Chapter IV. First, however, Chapter III will examine Frey's gift of *ár* more closely.

---

[24] This is the same Thorgrim whose mound is kept free of frost by Frey.

[25] Regal's translation ("Gisli Sursson's Saga" 20).

CHAPTER III

Ár:
Prosperity and
Abundance

One of the blessings brought by Frey and by all the "good kings" whose reigns echo the god's is *ár*. The word descends from Proto-IndoEuropean **yēr-* via Proto-Germanic **jeram*, both meaning "year" (Watkins 102). *Ár* means both a calendrical year and, more often, a "good year," especially in the agricultural or economic sense. It is often translated "good seasons" or "good harvest." Its opposite—often translated "want," "famine," and the like— is *hallæri*, which combines a form related to *ár* (*æri*) with an element (*hall*) based on the idea of leaning or swerving; it implies a year that has gone badly wrong and deviated from its normal, healthy state of *ár*.

Ár is also the name of the tenth rune in the Younger Futhark. The Norwegian *Rune Poem* describes it a gift of Frodhi, the semi-mythical king who is so closely associated with Frey himself[1]:

> *Ár* is good for men;
> I guess Frodhi was open-handed.

---

[1] The original text can be found in Halsall (182).

Ár: *Prosperity and Abundance*

The Icelandic *Rune Poem* begins the same way but gives a fuller description of *ár* itself[2]:

> *Ár* is good for men,
> and a good summer,
> and a thriving field.

In ancient Scandinavia, the year was divided into two seasons, summer and winter. In Iceland, summer began in (modern) April and ended in October. The major work of raising and harvesting crops as well as fattening the livestock for winter all occurred during the summer season, and a "good summer" was thus a productive one. Summer was also the "raiding and trading" season for the Vikings, so a "good summer" might also be one that was financially successful. In the third line of the Icelandic poem, the word translated "field" is *akr* (cognate to English "acre"). It means both a cultivated field and the crops growing in such a field. The adjective *algróinn* that modifies *akr* is related to the verb *gróa*, which means both "to grow" and (from the idea of a wound's growing together) "to heal"; one meaning of *algróinn* is "perfectly healed" (Cleasby and Vigfusson). So, the word implies, not only that the field is well-grown (i.e., that the harvest is good), but that the plants are healthy and strong. Dickins' choice of "thriving" to translate *algróinn* is a good one, and I have borrowed it in my translation above (31).

The Old English cognate of *ár* is *gēar*, and both words have similar semantic ranges. The variant form *gēr* is the name of the twelfth rune in the Anglo-Frisian Futhork, and the corresponding verse in the Old English *Rune Poem* shows that *gē(a)r*, like *ár*, often implies a productive and blessed year[3]:

---

[2] The original text can be found in Halsall (185).
[3] The original text can be found in Halsall (88).

> *Gēr* is the joy of men,   when God allows
> (holy king of the sky/heaven[4])   the ground to give
> excellent growth   to the powerful and the needy.

Despite the Christian overtones, the Old English poem again stresses the ideas of abundant harvest and of divine kingship (here assigned to "God," but of course the word *god* was originally used of any deity). The poem also emphasizes that a good year is a blessing to all people, regardless of rank. The word translated "joy" is *hiht*, which also means "hope, joyous expectation"; it is related to the verb *hyhtan*, "to hope, trust, look forward to with hope or joy" (Bosworth). So, there is a sense of joyful confidence associated with *gé(a)r*.

Thus, *ár* is a prosperous, successful year of good harvests that people look forward to with joy; the overall sense is one of unstinting abundance. These blessings are granted by a divine king/god. Preeminent among these provident rulers is Frey himself, whom Snorri explicitly calls *árguð*, "*ár*-god" (*Skáldskaparmál* 14).

Some additional evidence links Frey specifically with agricultural production. Snorri says that Frey rules over "the produce of the earth[5]" (*Gylfaginning* 24). Several places in Scandinavia are named **Freysakr*, "Frey's field," **Freysvin*, "Frey's meadow," and the like (Turville-Petre 168), and a field near a Frey's hof[6] in Iceland is named "Sure-Giver" (*Vitaðsgjafi*) "because it was never barren[7]" (*Víga-Glúms s.* 7). Scyld, the infant who arrives mysteriously by sea in *Beowulf* and founds the Scylding dynasty[8], is called *Scefing* (4), which means "son of *Scef* (sheaf)" or "of the sheaf." In

---

[4] Old English *heofon* originally meant the vault of the sky and was later extended to the Christian Heaven; both meanings are common in Anglo-Saxon texts.

[5] Faulkes' translation (Snorri *Edda* 24).

[6] Hof =a Norse temple.

[7] McKinnell's translation ("Killer-Glum's Saga" 277).

[8] See Chapter II.

Æthelweard's tenth-century chronicle, Scef is listed as Scyld's father (North 183), but the identities of Scyld and Scef (or the variant Sceaf) are conflated in the sources. Æthelweard himself describes Sceaf's early life in terms that parallel Scyld's in *Beowulf* and Ing's in the Old English *Rune Poem*: as a child, Sceaf arrives on an island in a boat and grows up to become king (qtd in Orchard 137). In some genealogies, the son of Scyld is named *Beow*, "barley" (North 183). Thus, Old English sources associate the sheaf of grain and barley itself with a mythical king who drifts in from the sea as a child.

In the Eddic poem *Lokasenna*, Frey himself is connected with barley. The prose introduction explains that one of Frey's servants is named "Byggvir." *Bygg* means "barley," and in the poem Loki sneers at Byggvir for "chattering under the quern" (44.4). Byggvir has sometimes been seen as the personification or spirit of barley itself. Lindow notes, "[M]uch of what the poem [*Lokasenna*] says of Byggvir can be imagined to fit barley, which is tiny, ground in a mill, and used in beer." He goes on to acknowledge, however, that such a personification would be "virtually unique in Scandinavian mythology" (91). I think it more likely that Byggvir, like the other servants of the gods mentioned in Norse lore, is an essentially humanlike figure. Dronke (343) and Orchard (29) translate his name as "barley-boy" and (tentatively) "corn-boy," respectively. If Byggvir's role is to assist with milling and brewing, his role becomes more parallel to that of Beyla (see below). This interpretation also makes comic sense of Byggvir's threat to grind Loki to a pulp (*Lokasenna* 43.3). Finally, if Byggvir's job is to help with the grain harvest, this adds sting to Loki's taunt, "You never knew how to apportion food among men" (46.1-2). Regardless of Byggvir's precise nature, the fact that he is Frey's servant unambiguously connects the god with barley.

Lokasenna also mentions a second servant of Frey named Beyla. The meaning of her name has been the subject of considerable debate, but Simek reports that the most widely-accepted theory relates "Beyla" to *baula*, cow (36). Loki calls Beyla *deigia*, "dairymaid," and also accuses her of being *öll... dritin*, "all shitty"—a probable result of working in the cow-barn (*Lokasenna* 56.4)! Ellis Davidson has pointed out the critical importance of milk as a food in the Scandinavian countries and has also noted that dairying was the province of women ("Milk" 92). Byggvir and Beyla thus associate Frey with two of the most important foods—grain and milk—produced by agriculture in Northern Europe.

Cattle produce not only milk but also meat. Less common in the average diet than grain or dairy products, meat was more highly valued and is the food generally mentioned in descriptions of ritual feasts. A discussion of its significance leads beyond simple agricultural production and "fertility." In this context, two food animals particularly associated with Frey—cattle and swine—are important.

The connection of Frey with cattle at first seems straightforward—they are frequent beasts of sacrifice. *Víga-Glúms saga* (9) tells of the sacrifice of an ox to Frey (the offering was evidently well-received; the tale is told more fully in Ch. IV below). In *Brandkrossa þáttur*, a man named Odd has a bull killed and cooked and then offers the entire feast to Frey[9] (1). Bull's blood and meat are offered to the *álfar* in *Kormáks saga* (22). Ottar, a devoted follower of Frey's sister Freyja, builds her an altar and reddens it with the blood of cattle (*Hyndluljóð* 10.3).

There are hints, however of a strange reversal in the roles of sacrificer and sacrificed. First, Snorri records in the *Þulur* that the name "Frey" can be used poetically to mean an ox (89), which could simply mean that the animal was particularly associated with the god or his strength. However, two incidents in which a king is gored to death by

---

[9] Turville-Petre notes that this tale "was written under the influence of *Víga-Glúms Saga*, but adds something to it" (256).

an ox under bizarre circumstances suggest that the beast could also act on behalf of the god as a sacred executioner.

The first example comes from *Ynglinga saga*. King Egil is one of the Yngling kings descended from Frey, and Snorri describes his violent death (26):

> It then befell in Sweden that an ox which was to be used for the offering [*til blóts*] had grown old and was overmuch fattened so that it became dangerous, and when they wanted to take it, it dashed to the wood [and] became mad... It once happened that when [King Egil] had ridden hunting with his men that he followed an animal for a long time and had ridden after it into the wood away from all his men. Then he came upon the ox... The king struck at it but his spear sheered off and the ox stuck its horns into the flank of the horse which straightway fell down flat and the king with him. The king then leaped up again and would draw his sword, but the ox stuck its horns into his breast so that they went deep in. Then the king's men came up and slew the ox, but the king lived only a short while and was buried in a howe near Upsala[10].

Many of the Yngling kings died unnatural deaths suggestive of sacrifice, but Egil's is the only case in which a "sacrificial" animal acts to sacrifice the king.

The second case involves the death of Frodhi, that semi-mythical king who comes up so often in this study of Frey. As reported by Saxo Grammaticus, an enemy of Frodhi's changes her shape into that of a "sea-cow[11]." When the king

---

[10] Translation by Monsen and Smith (Snorri *Heimskringla* 19).

[11] "Sea-cows" appear in an Icelandic folktale as especially fine beasts kept by mer-people called "marbendills." In the story, a farmer releases a marbendill he has caught while fishing; in return, he receives a splendid cow. "From her a great race of cattle is descended, that has since spread

approaches, the sea-cow "thrust her horn forward, charged the king and pierced one of his flanks. The gash took his life...[12]" (I.157). Afterwards, his body was preserved and carried around the countryside (see Ch. II above). Taken together, these odd stories suggest that cattle were associated with sacrifice, not just as victims, but also as divine agents who might take the lives of kings connected to Frey[13].

Cattle also represented abundance and wealth in Germanic cultures. The Norse word *fé* means both "cattle, livestock" and "money, riches"; it goes beyond the idea of "fertility" to include wealth in all its forms from living animals to cold hard cash. Frey and his father Njordh are strongly connected with the cattle/wealth concept denoted by *fé*. The Viking poet Egil Skalagrimmson says that Frey and Njordh have given his friend Arinbjorn *féar afli*, "wealth's power" (*Egils s.* 160). Snorri says that Frey is *fégjafa*, "wealth-giving," and governs *féscelu manna*, "the wealth-happiness of men" (*Skáldskaparmál* 14; *Gylfaginning* 24). The element *scela* in *féscelu* means "bliss, happiness," and *féscelu* thus suggests the ease and security that wealth can provide.

A second word for wealth, *auðr*, is also associated closely with the Vanir. In the case of Njordh, this connection was proverbial: in *Vatnsdœla saga*, a man is described as "rich as Njordh" [*auðigur sem Njörður*] (47), and Snorri calls the god Njordh *hinn auðga*, "the wealthy" (*Ynglinga s* 4). *Auðr* (unlike *fé*) is not normally applied to livestock, but

---

over all the land: grey in colour and called sea-cattle" (*Elves, Trolls, and Elemental Beings* 72-4).

[12] Fisher's translation.

[13] Turville-Petre (170) reports a variant of Saxo's story: "This same Fróði, according to Arngrímur Jónsson, was pierced by the antlers of a hart." Frey himself is armed with a hart's antler [*hjartarhorni*] when he kills the giant Beli (Snorri *Gylfaginning* 37), so the idea that the beast acts to sacrifice the king to the god could apply to this version of the story, also.

it does appear as the first element in the name of *Auðumla*[14], the great cow who was formed from the rime in Ginnungagap at the beginning of time and whose milk nourished the primordial giant Ymir[15] (*Gylfaginning* 6).

Wealth is also a striking feature of the reign of the ubiquitous Frodhi. Snorri states that "Frodhi's meal" is a kenning for "gold." He describes a myth in which King Frodhi sets two giantesses to work an enchanted mill and grind out "gold and peace [*frið*] and happiness" (*Skáldskaparmál* 52). Snorri then gives the text of the poem *Gróttasöngr*, in which the giantesses sing (5):

> Riches [*auð*] let us grind for Frodhi,
> grind complete happiness,
> grind plenty of wealth [*féar*]
> on the mill-box of gladness.
> Let him sit on riches [*auði*],
> let him sleep on down,
> let him wake to delight;
> then it's ground well.

In the myth of Frodhi's mill, the blessings of wealth are bound together with the idea of divine kingship represented by Frodhi/Frey.

Boars, like cattle, are closely associated with Frey. *Vaningi* ("of the Vanir"), a term applied to Frey in *Skírnismál* (37.4), could also be used poetically to mean a boar (Turville-Petre 255). According to Snorri, Frey owned a boar named *Gullinbursti*, "Golden-Bristled," that drew his chariot (*Gylfaginning* 49). Crafted by the dwarves, "it could run across sea and sky by night and day faster than any

---

[14] Thanks to Victorria Wytcherley for drawing this connection to my attention.

[15] Simek identifies the second element in Audhumla's name as *humala, "hornless" and interprets her name to mean "the hornless cow with lots (of milk)" (22).

horse, and it never got so dark […] that it was not bright enough wherever it went, there was so much light shed from its bristles[16]" (*Skáldskaparmál* 43). One version[17] of *The Saga of King Heidrek the Wise* describes a great boar dedicated to Frey:

> King Heidhrek made offerings [*blótaði*] to Frey. He would give Frey the greatest boar he could get. It was considered so holy that swearings about all important cases were made on its bristles, and the boar would be offered [*blóta*] at the sacrificial offering. On Yule Eve, the sacrificial boar was led into the hall before the king, and men laid their hands on its bristles and made binding vows.

Another text[18] of the same saga says that Heidhrek's boar "was as huge as the strongest fully-grown bulls, and so fair of coat that every hair seemed to be of gold[19]" (30-1), a description that recalls Frey's own boar, Gullinbursti. The practice of swearing oaths on a boar at Yule is also described in the prose text following verse 30 of *Helgakviða Hjörvarðssonar*.

The boar of Northern Europe, whether wild or (more-or-less) domesticated, was intelligent, prolific, and tough. A story from *Landnámabók* illustrates how boars were viewed in Norse culture (57). Ingimund the Old was one of Iceland's original settlers. He built a great hof to Frey on his land and

---

[16] Faulkes' translation (Snorri *Edda* 97).

[17] See Tolkien's edition of *The Saga of King Heidrek the Wise* for a discussion of the extant manuscripts (xxix-xxxi). The passage cited above comes from the "H" manuscript, not the "R" text preferred by most editors and generally considered closest to the (lost) original. Kershaw's translation (titled "The Saga of Hervör and Heithrek") includes considerable material from "H" (80), including the passage above (the translation shown is mine, however).

[18] The "R" version.

[19] Tolkien's translation.

was a successful and wealthy man. At one point, "Ingimund lost ten pigs, and when they were found the following autumn they numbered a hundred and twenty[20]." This prodigious increase in swine that have run wild is reported for other settlers as well, and it is always considered remarkable (42, 66). In Ingimund's case, when the settlers set out to catch the pigs, the herd-boar leapt into the water and swam so hard that "his hoofs came off. He died of exhaustion[21]" (57). Ingimund, an exceptional Freysman, owned a boar who was equally exceptional in both fecundity and fighting-spirit.

The fierce boar was also associated specifically with warriors and battle. Terms[22] for boar in the *Þulur* include *valglitnir*, "slaughter-shiner"; *valbassi*, "slaughter-bear"; and *vigrir* "warlike" (97). The dying hero Sigurdh boasts that, if his enemies had attacked while he was awake to defend himself, "It would have been more difficult for them to kill me than the fiercest wild bison or boar[23]" (*Völsunga s.* 30). The boar was a symbol of both aggression and protection. *Guðrúnarkviða II* describes how "Sigurdh's ships slipped from land, savage swine graven on the prows" (16.1-2). *Hildigöltr* ("battle-boar") is a term for "helmet" (*Þulur* 59), *Beowulf* describes helmets protected with boar images (303-6;1448-54), and Ellis Davidson describes archaeological finds, including several helmets and a sword, decorated with images of boars (*Myths* 49-50).

Thus, though the boar was renowned for his fertility, he was equally famed for his valor, and he has now carried us far afield from *ár*, from simple wealth and plenty. The mighty boar, whose likeness protects warriors and who receives the vows sworn at the sacred feast of Yule,

---

[20] Translation by Pálsson and Edwards (*Book of Settlements* 85).
[21] Translation by Pálsson and Edwards (85).
[22] Translations of the terms for boar are Faulkes' (Snorri *Edda* 164).
[23] Byock's translation (*Saga of the Volsungs* 90).

embodies not only vigor but holiness. Both are vital elements of Frey's gift of *friðr*, the subject of the next chapter.

CHAPTER IV

Friðr:
Sacred
Inviolability

Friðr is usually translated "peace," but the English word fails to convey the full force and range of *friðr*. Its meanings in Old Norse include "inviolability" and "sacredness" (Cleasby and Vigfusson), and it is cognate to other words in Germanic languages related to kinship, courtship, and freedom. Green makes sense of this constellation of meanings by tracing them to a root adjective that means "own" and was applied early in Germanic history to designate one's "own" kin or people (39-44). Marriage brought an outsider into one's own kin-group, and membership in the broader society became linked to the legal concept of freedom. In Germanic culture, the "free"—that is, those who were entitled to full rights by law—were legally inviolable. Inviolable did not mean invincible; rather, someone who was legally inviolable could not be killed with impunity, and the victim's family had the right to take revenge or receive compensation. In Old Norse, the word for this legal status is *helgi*, which also means "holiness." A sentence of outlawry ejected a man from the group and stripped him of his inviolability. The outlaw was termed *óhelgi*, "without *helgi*, unhallowed" and was said to forfeit *friðr*; he could now be killed with no legal consequences to the killer.

Thus, *friðr* refers primarily to the "peace" that exists *within* a group. As Green explains, *friðr* originally meant "the state or condition prevailing amongst those who regard each other as their own kindred" (43); furthermore, this "[p]eace in the pre-Christian sense was not simply a passive state (the absence of hostilities), but an active one (a readiness to help and defend one another)" (60). As society became more complex and was influenced, first by the Roman idea of *pax*, and later by the Christian ideal of peace, the meaning of *friðr* "expanded to embrace the community at large, the king's peace" (43). *Friðr* remained, however, concerned with "the rule of law [and] upholding internal peace." Green reports that its Old High German cognate *fridu* frequently meant "'protection, help' rather than 'peace'." In addition, the range of meanings of both *friðr* and *helgi* show that this state of internal harmony and mutual protection was viewed as sacred.

Norse literature speaks of a mythical, golden age the when entire nations achieved the holy state of *friðr*. This time was called the *Fróðafriðr* ("*friðr* of Frodhi"). According to Snorri's *Ynglinga saga*, the *Fróðafriðr* began during Frey's reign, and "the Swedes attributed it to Frey" (10), but most of the surviving stories focus on King Frodhi himself. Saxo explains that Frodhi, after years of hard campaigning, has achieved for his Danes such a "reputation for shining bravery[1]" that he is now able "to unleash his severity against thefts and robberies, as these were evils of an internal, domestic nature" (I.156). Frodhi's efforts are so successful that, when he sets up a gold ring at a crossroad, "Frothi's royal authority was so influential that the gold, to be had for the taking, was preserved as if behind steel bars"

---

[1] All translations of Saxo in this paragraph are Fisher's.

(I.156). In *Gróttasöngr*, the giantesses grind out, not only wealth, but also *friðr* for Frodhi (6):

> Here shall no-one
> harm another,
> nor plan to wound him,
> nor work his death,
> nor strike with sharpened
> sword—not even
> if bound he finds
> his brother's killer.

This state of world-wide *friðr* would have seemed miraculous to the poet's audience. In the Heathen world, blood-vengeance was a duty, and violence was commonplace. In the 1st century C.E., Tacitus wrote that the Germanic tribes "proceed to business or just as often banquets, always of course under arms. To drink away the day and night disgraces no one. Brawls are frequent, as is normal among the intoxicated, and seldom end in mere abuse, but more often in slaughter and bloodshed[2]" (86). The only exception was during the procession of the Vanic goddess Nerthus: "They do not begin wars, they do not take up arms; everything iron is shut away; peace and tranquility are only then known and only then loved[3]" (93). A thousand years later, the situation had changed little: the Eddic poem *Hávamál* advises (38):

> From his weapons
> a man in the field
> should not stir a step;
> he can't know for certain
> when spear he'll need

---

[2] Rives' translation.
[3] Rives' translation.

out on the open road.

Thus, to establish the *Fróðafriðr* would have required a king/god of extraordinary strength, a warrior so powerful that none dared violate his sacred *friðr*.

In ordinary society, *friðr* rarely extended to whole nations, but it was nonetheless expected in places and times of special sanctity. Shedding blood in anger, and in some cases even bearing arms, was forbidden both at the Thing (the regular assembly of free men) and in temples (hofs).

The Thing is a central feature of public life in all periods of Germanic history. The sacred origins and rites of the Thing are discussed in detail by Baetke (150-4). In Scandinavia, a priest (*goði*) was called upon to open the Thing by establishing *þinghelgi*; this sacred state of inviolability was in force during the whole period of the assembly. The idea of *þinghelgi* occurs frequently in Norse sources, most often in expressions of horror when it is violated. In *Eyrbyggja saga*, for example, after a fight breaks out during the Thing, the traditional site for the meeting must be abandoned because it has been "defiled by blood spilt in rage[4]," and a new site is established (20). The medieval law code *Westgötalag* calls slaying someone at the Thing *niþingsværk*, the act of a vile and utterly despicable person (qtd in Baetke 151). This collective horror at the sacrilege of violence at the Thing probably contributed to the prohibition of weapons in later periods: Tacitus says of the assembly in early times that "none of this business, either public or private, will they conduct except under arms[5]" (82), but by the Viking Age, carrying weapons was forbidden at many Things in Scandinavia (e.g., *Egils s.* 57).

The temporary state of *friðr* that was established at the Thing was in perpetual force within the sacred precincts of a

---

[4] Quinn's translation ("The Saga of the People of Eyri" 137).
[5] Rives' translation.

hof. *Egils saga* tells of a ritual feast [*blót*] where everyone was unarmed because they were within a hof, which was holy and inviolate [*hofshelgi*] (49). In defiance of this prohibition, a man brings a sword into the hof and kills an enemy; because of this crime, he is immediately declared an outlaw [*vargar*[6]]. In *Vatnsdæla saga*, carrying weapons into a hof dedicated to Frey is prohibited because it would bring down "the wrath of the gods" (17). *Víga-Glúms saga* tells how the hero Glum, who harbors an outlaw, must do it in secret: "outlawed men were not supposed to be there, because Frey, to whom the temple there was dedicated, did not allow it[7]" (19).

The word usually used to describe the prohibition on carrying weapons of war at the Thing or in the hof is *vápnlauss*, "weaponless." Snorri uses the same word to describe Frey himself when the god defeats the giant Beli armed only with a stag's antler, though Snorri adds, "It did not matter much[...] Freyr could have killed him with his fist[8]" (*Gylfaginning* 37). In *Lokasenna*, Loki mocks Frey for having given up his sword, which he will miss come Ragnarok (42.2-4). The mythological explanation is found in the poem *Skírnismál*, which tells of Frey's love for the giant-woman Gerdh. To persuade his servant Skirnir to act as his emissary to her, Frey gives Skirnir his sword and his horse (8-9). Both are princely gifts. The sword is magical and can fight on its own; the mighty horse will carry a rider even through flame. Snorri identifies Frey's horse as the stallion *Blóðughófi*, "bloody-hoof," who is listed among the steeds of great warriors (*Skáldskaparmál* 72).

Frey's surrender of sword and steed is an extraordinary act for a warrior, for whom a famous weapon and mighty

---

[6] *Vargr* literally means a savage wolf; the term is often applied to outlaws, who, like wolves in the forest, were outside the bounds of society.
[7] McKinnell's translation ("Killer-Glum's Saga" 297).
[8] Faulke's translation (Snorri *Edda* 32).

stallion were standard equipment. Sigurdh, the greatest hero of Northern myth, owns a horse (Grani) and sword (Gram) as eminent as himself; both have come to him through the efforts of the god Odhin, and Grani, like Blodhughofi, is willing to cross a barrier of flame (*Völsunga saga*). Various theories have been advanced to explain Frey's willingness to give up his horse and weapon. However, I think the most likely explanation is connected to *friðr* and the prohibition on weapons in holy places. More specifically, the fact that Frey is *vápnlauss* connects him to taboos that applied to *goðar* ("priests"), especially the *Freysgoðar* who served the god himself. First, Frey himself is described as a priest of the gods. In *Sörla þáttur*, he and his father Njordh are described as "sacrifice-priests [*blótgoðar*]" (1). In *Ynglinga saga*, Snorri calls Frey's sister Freyja *blótgyðja*, "sacrifice-priestess," and also says that Frey and Njordh are *díar með Ásum*, "priests among the gods" (4). The word *díar* is unusual, and Turville-Petre suggests that Snorri chose this word to indicate "priests of a particularly exalted kind" (163). These references suggest that the Vanir may have had a special sacral role among the gods. Second, certain human priests, like Frey, did not carry weapons or ride stallions. The Venerable Bede writes that, for Coifi, the Heathen "Chief Priest" of Anglo-Saxon Northumbria, "It had not been lawful... to carry arms or to ride anything but a mare[9]" (130). On converting to Christianity, Coifi arms himself and mounts a stallion; when he reaches the temple, "he cast into it the spear he carried and thus profaned it[10]." In *Flateyjarbók*, the Christian king Olaf Tryggvason sets out to desecrate a hof in Trondheim. Outside it, he sees a stud of horses and is told that they belong to Frey. Olaf mounts the stallion, rides it into the hof, and tears down the idol of Frey (1: 401).

---

[9] Sherley-Price's translation.
[10] Sherley-Price's translation.

The stallion desecrated by Olaf was dedicated to Frey, and other evidence confirms that particular horses were considered sacred to the gods, especially to Frey. Tacitus writes that, to divine the future, the Germanic tribes interpreted the sounds made by sacred horses who are "maintained at public expense in the groves and woods. They are white and untouched by any earthly task... [the people] see themselves as mere servants of the gods, but the horses as their intimates[11]" (81). In *Vatnsdæla saga*, a man called Brand owns a horse named Freyfaxi, "Frey-mane" (34). The horse is exceptionally brave and strong, and the saga says that "Brand placed special faith in Faxi[12]." In *Hrafnkels saga Freysgoða*, Hrafnkel, a priest of Frey, owns a splendid stallion, again named Freyfaxi. The hero dedicates half of Freyfaxi to Frey and swears an oath to kill anyone who rides the horse (3). Later, Hrafnkel is driven from his land, and his enemies kill Freyfaxi and say, "It would be most fitting that he who owns him should take him[13]" (15). Their tone is sarcastic, but a memory of ritual sacrifice may lie behind the incident.

Other evidence shows that horses were sacrificed and eaten at ritual feasts. When Iceland converted to Christianity, Heathens were allowed to keep up some of their practices as a pragmatic compromise between the followers of the old and new faiths. According to Ari Thorgilsson, eating the flesh of horses was one of the few Heathen customs that was specifically permitted to continue (Byock *Medieval Iceland* 142). Snorri's *Hákonar saga Aðalsteinsfóstra* shows the importance of this act. Raised as a Christian in England, King Hakon was forced by the Heathen people of Norway to consume horseflesh as part of his sacral duties as their king (17-18). At the annual autumn sacrifice, the assembled freemen demanded that the king partake of the horsemeat

---

[11] Rives' translation.
[12] Wawn's translation ("Saga of the People of Vatnsdal" 45).
[13] Gunnell's translation ("Saga of Hrafnkel Frey's Godi" 275).

that was being eaten at the feast. Hakon refused, but the people persisted, and he finally agreed to gape over the vessel where the meat had been boiled. This was not really acceptable to the worthy Heathens, and, at a Yule feast, they finally pressured the king into eating some horse-liver. Thus, not only were particular horses held sacred and inviolate in Germanic culture, but the ritual consumption of horseflesh was essential to Heathen religious practice.

As mentioned above, Hrafnkel swears an oath to kill anyone who rides Freyfaxi, the horse he shares with Frey. The seriousness of Hrafnkel's oath is made clear when the prohibition is violated: a farmhand named Einar rides Freyfaxi, and Hrafnkel regretfully takes his life: "Why did you ride the horse that you were forbidden to ride...? I would have forgiven you this one time if I had not sworn such a serious oath... [but] nothing goes well for people when the words of an oath come down on them[14]" (*Hrafnkels s. Freysgoða* 6). Hrafnkel, priest of Frey, has no choice but to fulfill his vow, and other sources also connect the god with the upholding of oaths. As described in Chapter III, Yule-oaths were sworn on a boar that was sacrificed to Frey. According to Orchard (121), an oath-swearing formula recorded in some versions of *Landnámabók* and *Ólafs saga Tryggvasonar* invokes Frey, Njordh, and the "all-powerful god." It seems that oaths, like *friðr*, are sacred to Frey.

Two stories illustrate the implacability of the god when the realm of the sacred that lies under his protection is desecrated. The first comes from Saxo Grammaticus (I.29-30). On a whim, the hero Hading kills a sea-creature while swimming. A woman then appears to him and says that he has killed a sacred being and will suffer disasters on land and sea until he appeases the gods. Her words are fulfilled: Hading's ships are destroyed by storms, and the house where

---

[14] Gunnell's translation ("Saga of Hrafnkel Frey's Godi" 265).

he takes shelter collapses. His terrible luck continues, and (I.30):

> There was no alleviation for his calamities till he had been able to atone for his wickedness by religious offerings... [He made] a holy sacrifice of dark-colored victims to the god Frø [= Frey]. He repeated this mode of propitiation at an annual festival and left it to be imitated by his descendants. The Swedes call it Frøblot[15].

Here, it seems that slaying the creature has deeply offended Frey, who causes the very elements to turn against Hading until the hero makes amends.

The second example is more subtle. In *Víga-Glúms saga*, the eponymous hero enjoys supernatural protection symbolized by a spear and cloak[16]. While thus warded, Glum transgresses against Frey in three ways. First, he slays his neighbor Sigmund in the field "Sure-Giver" that is adjacent to a hof of Frey and, it is implied, is encompassed within the *friðr* of the hof (8). Second, Glum secretly harbors an outlaw, which again violates Frey's laws and taints the holiness [*helgi*] of the hof and its precincts (19). Finally, the hero intentionally swears a deceptive oath on a sacred ring inside the hof itself (25).

While Glum is repeatedly offending Frey in this way, Sigmund's kinsman Thorkel, who has been driven from his land at Thvera by Glum, has gone to Frey's hof to make an offering (9):

> "Oh Frey," he said, "you who have long been my trust, and have received many oblations from me

---

[15] Fisher's translation.
[16] This protection may come from his own, powerful ancestors, from whom he inherited the tokens along with the family *hamingja* ("luck"), or it may come from Odhin himself.

and repaid them well, now I give you this ox, to the end that Glum may depart from the land at Thvera under a compulsion no less than that by which I go now. And let there now appear some token of whether you have accepted my offer or not."

And the ox started violently, bellowed and fell down dead, and it seemed to Thorkel that that was a good sign, and he was calmer in his mind, now that he thought that his offer had been accepted[17].

Glum nonetheless prospers and seems to have escaped the consequences of his acts. Then, he makes the fatal mistake of giving away his spear and cloak and with them the special protection that he has enjoyed. It seems that this frees Frey to act: almost immediately, Glum has this dream (26):

[H]e dreamed that large numbers of people had come to Thvera to meet Frey, and that he saw a large crowd on the gravel banks beside the river, while Frey sat on a throne. He dreamed that he asked who had come there.

They replied: "These are your bygone kinsmen, and now we're asking Frey that you may not be driven off the land at Thvera, but it's no use, for Frey answers curtly and angrily and remembers now Thorkel the Tall's gift of an ox[18]."

Soon afterwards, Glum loses his farm and is forced to move repeatedly. He never again achieves success or prosperity. In

---

[17] McKinnell's translation ("Killer-Glum's Saga" 282).
[18] McKinnell's translation (308).

other words, *ár* and *friðr* are denied to him for the rest of his life.

CHAPTER V

Sex and
Sensuality

The main connotations of *friðr* were discussed at length in Chapter IV, but the word also carries yet another meaning. *Friðr* can be translated "love," and it is related to the words *friðla*, "mistress" (in the sexual sense), and *friðgin*, "lovers" (Cleasby and Vigfusson). Because Frey is so closely associated with *friðr*, these erotic connotations suggest that Frey may also be concerned with human sexuality. Unfortunately, most of the surviving information about Norse myth and culture was recorded by medieval Christians who are frustratingly reticent on this subject. For example, Uppsala in Sweden was a major center of Frey's cult, and Adam of Bremen provides graphic descriptions of the animal and human sacrifices performed there. When it comes to the (possible) sexual element in these rites, however, Adam turns squeamish and tells us only, "Furthermore, the incantations customarily chanted in the ritual of a sacrifice of this kind are manifold and unseemly; therefore, it is better to keep silence about them[1]" (208). Saxo is equally censorious and little more informative; his hero Starkather leaves Uppsala because he is "disgusted [with] the womanish body movements, the clatter of actors on the stage and the soft

---

[1] Tschan's translation.

tinkling of bells[2]" (I.172). Saxo adds approvingly, "A manly individual is resistant to wantonness[3]" (I.172).

Fortunately, some information did escape the censors. Adam of Bremen describes the idols at Uppsala as follows (207-8):

> In this temple, entirely decked out in gold, the people worship the statues of three gods... Thor, they say, presides over the air, which governs the thunder and lightning, the winds and rains, fair weather and crops. The other, Wotan—that is, the Furious—carries on war and imparts to man strength against his enemies. The third is Frikko[4], who bestows peace and pleasure on mortals. His likeness, too, they fashion with an immense phallus... If plague or famine threaten, a libation is poured to the idol Thor; if war, to Wotan; if marriages are to be celebrated, to Frikko[5].

Interestingly, Adam identifies Thor as the primary god of fertility; Frey's province in this text is specifically "pleasure."

Another hint of Frey's sexual nature is the association of the Vanir with incest. Snorri's *Ynglinga saga* records that Frey is the son of Njordh and Njordh's (unnamed) sister (4). In *Lokasenna*, Loki confirms that Njordh and his sister are Frey's parents (36.3) and also accuses Freyja of copulating with her brother Frey[6] (32.3). The word "Vanir" itself

---

[2] Fisher's translation.

[3] Fisher's translation.

[4] "Frikko" is generally identified as Frey. Simek favors **friðlan*, "lover," as the probable root of "Frikko" (93). **Friðlan* is presumably cognate to *friðr*.

[5] Tschan's translation.

[6] Snorri notes that the Vanir abandoned their custom of brother-sister incest when they came to Asgardh (*Ynglinga s.* 4).

descends from a Proto-IndoEuropean root **wen-* meaning "to desire, strive for"; the same root gave rise to the name of Venus, the Roman goddess of passion (Watkins 98).

All this information is suggestive, but the clearest evidence for Frey's sexual nature comes from the Eddic poem *Skírnismál*. This poem contains the only major myth about Frey that has survived, and it tells of the god's desperate, consuming desire for the giant-maiden Gerdh. Having glimpsed her from afar, Frey is sick with love for her, and he sends his servant Skirnir to court her for him. Gerdh agrees to wed Frey in nine nights' time, and the poem ends with the anguished cry of the ardent lover (42):

> Long is a night,
> long are two,
> how can I endure three?
> Often a month
> to me seemed less
> than half these nights of waiting.

The poem has one aspect that is disturbing to modern readers: to compel her agreement, Skirnir threatens Gerdh first with violence (a threat she scornfully defies), and then with an elaborate and terrible curse: she will become hideous and be cast down below the gates of Hel. Food will become loathsome to her, and she will be given goat's piss to drink. She will be afflicted with weeping and grief and seized by lust and madness. She will be denied the company, sight, and sound of men and instead will be given to the loathsome giants called "thurses." The same word (*Þurs*) is the name of the third rune in the Younger Futhark, and both the Norwegian and Icelandic *Rune Poems* call it the "torment of women." Skirnir ends his curse by invoking the *þurs* rune itself (36):

> Thurs [*Þurs*] I rist you,

and three staves –
lust [*ergi*] and raving [*œði*]
and unbearable need [*óþola*].

The "three staves" invoked by Skirnir all suggest sexual torment. When applied to women, *ergi* seems to indicate something like nymphomania. *Œði* means "madness, frenzy"; it is related to the name of Odhin, god of the berserker rage. *Óþola* literally means (something that is) "unbearable, unendurable." The entire curse seems directed at first inducing intolerable desire and then answering it with nothing, or worse.

An analogous situation is described in *Brennu-Njáls saga* (6-7): a curse incites sexual desire that literally cannot be satisfied. Hrut, an Icelander, travels to Norway and has an affair with Queen Gunnhild. The following spring, Hrut wants to return to Iceland and his fiancée Unn, but he lies to Gunnhild and denies that he has a woman waiting for him at home. Gunnhild sees through him and, offended that Hrut "did not trust [her] with the truth," says, "I place this spell on you: you will not have any sexual pleasure with the woman you plan to marry in Iceland, though you'll be able to enjoy yourself with other women[7]." Hrut marries Unn, but the marriage is unhappy, and eventually Unn tells her father the cause: "When he comes close to me his penis is so large that he can't have any satisfaction from me, and yet we've both tried every possible way to enjoy each other, but nothing works[8]."

The coercion of Gerdh in *Skírnismál* has odd parallels in the life of King Frodhi (again!). Saxo Grammaticus describes two weddings of the king with reluctant maidens. In the first episode, the king sends emissaries to the princess Hanuda, but she "disdained Frothi[9]" (I.120). Gotvara, wife of one of

---

[7] Cook's translation ("Njal's Saga" 9).
[8] Cook's translation (11).
[9] All translations of Saxo in this paragraph are by Fisher.

Frodhi's counsellors, gives the maiden a "love-potion [that] turned the girl's inflexibility to desire, destroyed her prejudice and substituted erotic passion" (I.120). Love-potion notwithstanding, the marriage ends badly, and Frodhi sends a new group of emissaries to court a second wife for him. A woman in the party gives the latest prospect "a drink mixed with something which channeled the girl's desires into love for Frothi" (I.139).

In these stories, Frey and Frodhi win reluctant women through magic that arouses lust so strong it is "unbearable." I suggest that the magical runes and potions in these stories represent Frey's power to awaken the chaotic force that is sexual desire. In Heathen Scandinavia, marriages were viewed as family alliances, and uncontrolled desire threatened social norms. Romantic love was dangerous—so dangerous that a man who composed love-poetry [*mansöngr*] about a woman could be outlawed for it (Foote and Wilson 112). *Man* means a bondservant or slave, so *mansöngr* suggests that the verses create a kind of thralldom or compulsion. Snorri says of Frey's sister Freyja, renowned for her sexual nature and magical skills, that "[s]he was very fond of love songs [*mansöngr*]. It is good to pray to her concerning love affairs[10]" (*Gylfaginning* 24).

The life of Ingolf in *Vatnsdæla saga* demonstrates how passion could wreak havoc on the social order. Ingolf, grandson of the eminent Frey's man Ingimund the Old, is the "best-looking of men" (37); a verse about him describes how all women yearn for him (38). His great love is Valgerdh[11], the daughter of his neighbor Ottar. Ottar, alas, does not approve. Ingolf writes Valgerdh (illegal) love poems [*mansöngsvísur*] (37) and continues to visit Valgerdh despite a legal settlement that stipulates that if he does so he will

---

[10] Faulkes' translation (Snorri *Edda* 24).
[11] The feeling was apparently mutual; the saga describes how Valgerdh initiated their first conversation and later made fine clothes for Ingolf (37-8).

forfeit his legal inviolability and may be killed with impunity (39). Inevitably, the situation escalates, and three men, including Ingolf's brother Gudhbrand, end up dead because of Ingolf's obsession with Valgerdh.

In Viking society, love was thus a form of insanity that could lead to turmoil and bloodshed. For a high-ranking woman, "magic" would both explain and excuse her yielding to this dangerous madness. In Hanuda's case, at least, some excuse would have been necessary: Hanuda initially rejects Frodhi because he has not yet earned "worldly reputation[12]" and suffers from "want of renown[13]" (Saxo I.120). In other words, she marries beneath her, and some explanation of her rash choice is needed.

Gerdh's situation is more nuanced and more complex; she is not simply drugged into a state where Frey seems irresistible. However, there are hints in *Skírnismál* that her union with Frey was in some way socially forbidden. Early in the poem, Frey laments, "Of gods and elves, not one is willing that we should be together" (7.3-4). After she has agreed to wed Frey, Gerdh comments, "I had intended never to grant that I would love one of the Vanir well" (37.3-4). And, when Skirnir first arrives, Gerdh has an odd foreboding and fears that her "brother's bane" may be outside (16.3-4). Does this mean that Frey has killed her brother, and has that act created enmity between their families? There is also a subtle implication in *Skírnismál* that Gerdh may in fact desire Frey; after she agrees to the wedding, she names the time and place and says "there to the son of Njordh will Gerdh grant love-play [*gamans*]" (39.3-4). *Gaman* means "love, pleasure" but also "game, sport"; by using it, Gerdh may be issuing Frey an invitation, and perhaps also a challenge…

---

[12] Fisher's translation.
[13] Fisher's translation.

But what of the curse? It is never fulfilled; the threat alone is sufficient excuse for Gerdh to join with Frey. But, its nature is nonetheless revealing: it promises both to excite "unbearable need" and to deny its satisfaction. To reject Frey, it warns, is to be painfully deprived of good food, good drink, good sex, and good company—all the pleasures that Frey provides.

CHAPTER VI

Frey,
God of the World

So far, this work has considered how Frey was worshipped and understood by Heathens in the past. One key to that understanding is the concept of divine kingship. However, I am a practicing Heathen in the 21st century, and I have no desire to live under a monarch, divine or otherwise. So, I have a personal interest in the final question I will address in this work: what is Frey's role in a post-modern world?

To begin with, it is helpful to examine more closely the nature of kingship and how it changed over time in the Germanic world. In Tacitus' day, authority lay principally with the assembly of free men, though some had more influence than others (81-2):

> The leading men take counsel over minor issues, the major ones involve them all; yet even those decisions that lie with the commons are considered in advance by the élite... [At the assembly] the king or leading man is given a hearing, more through his influence in persuasion than his power in command... Likewise in these assemblies are chosen the leaders who administer justice in the cantons and hamlets[1].

---

[1] Rives' translation.

Over time, as the authority of the king became more permanent and also wider in scope, it also became his responsibility to maintain *friðr*. A skaldic poem praising a chieftain calls him "suppressor of robbers[2]" (Snorri *Skáldskaparmál* 79), and *Vellekla*, a poem by Einar Helgason lauding Jarl Hakon's rule in Norway, says that no one except Frodhi ever achieved such *friðr* on earth (18).

Guaranteeing *ár*—the prosperity on which the people's lives depended—was even more vital than maintaining *friðr*. And, the king's function as provider of *ár* was essentially sacral: he made sure that hofs were maintained and sacrifices performed. If he were derelict in this duty, the crops might fail, and the king would be blamed. Olaf Tree-feller "did not give many blood offerings and the Swedes liked that ill and thought that bad seasons [*hallænð*] came through it[3]"; when a famine did come, the Swedes offered up Olaf himself (Snorri *Ynglinga s.* 43).

Snorri provides a dramatic example of the relationship between the king's conduct and the health of the land. When the Christian sons of Erik Bloodaxe came to power in Norway, "they could do nothing to make the men of the land Christians; but wherever they came they broke down temples and destroyed the sacrifice [*blótum*][4]" (*Haraldar s. gráfeldar* 2). To make matters worse, Erik's sons were greedy and had little respect for the law. The results were dire: "there was great want [*hallæri*] in the land and the longer they ruled the more it grew. The bonders blamed the kings for it... So bad it became that the land folk well-nigh lacked everywhere corn and fish... and the snow lay over all the land in the middle of summer[5]" (16). Erik's sons were finally ousted by Jarl Hakon, who told the people to once again "keep up the temples and blood offering [*blótum*] all over the land, and so

---

[2] Faulkes' translation.
[3] Translation by Monsen and Smith (Snorri *Heimskringla* 32).
[4] Translation by Monsen and Smith (103-4).
[5] Translation by Monsen and Smith (Snorri *Heimskringla* 113).

it was done[6]" (*Ólafs s. Tryggvasonar* 16). The land now prospered: the herring returned, the corn flourished, and "the earth became green, as before" (Einar Helgason, *Vellekla* 16).

Though it was the king's responsibility to maintain *ár* and *friðr*, the Thing retained some of its ancient authority in Scandinavia and could influence, depose, or even (as we have seen) sacrifice an unsatisfactory king. As described above[7], King Hakon is pressured into eating horsemeat (i.e., into participating fully in the sacrificial rite), and Kings Olaf Tree-feller and Domaldi are sacrificed when the crops fail. In *The Saga of King Heidrek the Wise*, a Christian named Ingi becomes king of Sweden and suppresses Heathenism (62). At the Thing, the Heathen Swedes confront him with a choice: that he uphold their ancient laws and ways, or else relinquish the kingship. When Ingi refuses to renounce Christianity, the people hurl stones at him and drive him from the assembly. Ingi's kinsman Svein offers to perform sacrifice (*blót*) for the Swedes if they will take him as king; they gladly accept him, and a horse is immediately sacrificed and eaten at the Thing (63).

As kings continued to consolidate their power, the old social structures were eroded. In Norway, King Harald Fairhair ruthlessly extended his royal authority, and the newly-discovered country of Iceland was settled (or so at least the settlers' descendants believed) by those who refused to suffer Harald's tyranny and sought a new life elsewhere[8]. Those settlers chose to establish a republic based on the ancient tradition of the assembly: Iceland had no king and governed itself entirely through a system of Things.

---

[6] Translation by Monsen and Smith (125).
[7] Chapters IV and II, respectively.
[8] The actual reasons for the Settlement were doubtless more complex and varied, but it nonetheless significant that the Icelanders themselves believed that their ancestors had fled royal despotism.

The case of Iceland thus provides, at last, a way to approach the question posed at the beginning of this chapter: what is Frey's role in a land that has no king? Frey himself was certainly known and loved in Iceland. One of the most prominent chieftains in Iceland at the end of the settlement period was Thordh *Freysgoði*, "Frey's priest," and his descendants were called the *Freysgyðlingar*, "Frey's priestlings" (*Landnámabók* 84, 87, 102). As discussed in Ch. II, Thorgrim Thorsteinsson[9] was so close to Frey that the god kept his grave-mound free of frost. Other Icelanders whose devotion to Frey has already been noted are Hrafnkel *Freysgoði* and Thorkel the Tall, whose prayer for justice Frey answered in *Víga-Glúms saga*.

The life of another settler and Frey's-man, Ingimund the Old, is especially informative. The story is told in *Landnámabók* and more fully in *Vatnsdœla saga*. As is often true for medieval Icelandic writings, the two sources are not independent, but they are at least reassuringly consistent, which suggests that there was a single, accepted tradition for the story.

Ingimund's tale begins in Norway. A seeress predicts that Ingimund will make his home in Iceland, and "as a proof she said that something had vanished from his purse and wouldn't be found till he started digging for his high-seat pillars in the new country[10]" (*Landnámabók* 56). The "something" is a silver image of Frey, and Ingimund then consults a pair of shamans who describe the valley where it lies. Ingimund forcefully declares his intention never to settle in Iceland, but the seeress' words prey on his mind, and at last he consults King Harald of Norway (*Vatnsdœla s.* 12):

Ingimund said to the king, "I have in mind what the Lapp woman prophesied for me about a change in

---

[9] Turville-Petre notes that Thorgrim is also given the title *Freysgoði*, albeit "in a somewhat untrustworthy text" (166).

[10] Translation by Pálsson and Edwards (*Book of Settlements* 83).

my life, because I have no wish that it should ever be the case that I leave my family estate."

The king answered, "I cannot deny that the prophesy may have some purpose, and that Frey might wish his amulet to come to rest in the place where he wants his seat of honour to be established[11]."

Ingimund takes the king's advice and travels to Iceland. He recognizes the place described by the shamans. As his party approaches it, they see "good land with grass and wood. It was lovely to behold; people's faces brightened[12]" (15). The land proves to be as good as it looks—sheep can even survive the winter out-of-doors. Ingimund builds a great hof to Frey there and, as foretold, finds his lost image of the god when he sets up his high-seat pillars. Once he finds the amulet, Ingimund says, "It is indeed true to say that one cannot fight against fate, and we may now settle here in good spirits. This farm will be called Hof[13]."

Ingimund prospers at Hof and becomes one of the great men of the district. Interestingly, his character as described in the saga echoes that of the god he worships: Ingimund is handsome and athletic, "not at all aggressive towards lesser men, but tough and combative with his enemies[14]" (7). He is also open-handed: "the more plentiful his provisions, the more he engaged in gift-giving and other generous acts[15]." Ingimund, blessed by Frey, emulates him in sharing those blessings with his community.

As for Frey himself, King Harald's words suggest that the god intended to go to Iceland and be honored in the new

---

[11] Wawn's translation ("The Saga of the People of Vatnsdal" 16).
[12] Wawn's translation (20).
[13] Wawn's translation (20).
[14] Wawn's translation (10).
[15] Wawn's translation (11).

land. In Iceland, no king was needed to mediate the blessings of *ár* and *friðr*—they flowed directly from the god. Frey himself granted prosperity to his followers and punished those who desecrated his holy places with bloodshed or false oaths. He remained associated with burial mounds and ancestors, but they were now the howes of his followers and the family ancestors of the settlers of Iceland.

The god of Swedish kings and Icelandic farmers is the same god revered by Heathens today. In a world where kings have little place, shining Frey is still the *veraldargoð*, the god of the world. With open hands he offers abundance, protection, and pleasure to those who honor him.

> Frey is the best
> of all the bold
> riders in Asgardh's realm;
> he makes no wife
> nor maiden weep,
> and frees every captive from fetters.

—Lokasenna 37

The Functions
of Dumézil

Georges Dumézil, the 20th-century scholar of comparative religion, is best-known for his ideas about the tripartite structure of Indo-European religion and society. In the myths of various Indo-European cultures, Dumézil found evidence for three "functions" that were expressed both in the organization of social classes and the structure of the pantheon. He summarizes these functions as "magic and juridical sovereignty, physical force, fecundity" (*Gods* 118). For the Germanic peoples, Dumézil recognized the erosion of the tripartite social structure, but in the divine realm he confidentally assigned Odhin and Tyr to the First Function, Thor to the Second, and the Vanir (Frey, Njordh, and Freyja) to the Third. Of the Vanir, especially Frey, he says, "Even if it exceptionally occurs that they must be or do something else, [they] are first and foremost rich and givers of riches; they are patrons of fecundity and of pleasure…, also of peace" (3). Any anomalous data, such as Thor's power to fertilize the fields, he dismisses as "problems of detail" (5).

In one sense, I agree with him. Dumézil's interest was primarily in *origins*, in the structure of the ancestral Indo-European religion, and he used the surviving myths of various cultures to illuminate those origins much as a linguist uses words in modern languages to reconstruct ancient tongues. In *Mitra-Varuna*, he explains his approach (18):

[L]et no one reproach me with having according excessive importance to elements that in later stages of a religion are secondary and, as it were, fossilized; it was precisely my task to throw some light upon the old and superseded states.

In this context, his arguments that Frey descends from a Third Function deity of the Indo-Europeans remain convincing.

In his later work, however, Dumézil himself recognized that to understand how a religion functioned as a living tradition required more than an excavation of its origins. In *Archaic Roman Religion*, he expressed this more nuanced view (xvi-xvii):

It is not enough to extract from early Roman religion the pieces which can be explained by the religions of other Indo-European peoples... One must put them back in place, or rather leave them *in situ*, in the total picture and observe how they behaved in the different periods of Roman religion, how they survived, or perished, or became changed... [O]ne must consider Rome and its religion in themselves, for themselves, as a whole.

As for Roma, so for Germania. For Germanic religion "in itself," the concept of Frey as a Third Function deity is more hindrance than help in understanding how he was viewed by those who worshipped him. Two major developments in Germanic culture caused Frey to add aspects of the First and Second Functions to his original Third Function traits. First, society became highly militarized, and the Second Function of the warrior lost its restriction to one god or class and instead came to encompass all of society. Second, Frey seems to have assumed—at least in some times and places—many of the

First Function characteristics Dumézil identifies for gods and kings of the "Mitra" type.

The effects of militarization on Germanic society were apparent to Dumézil: "war invaded all, colored everything" (*Gods* 42). He comments on the virtual disappearance of the priestly class that represents the First Function in other Indo-European societies (e.g., the brahmans of India). On the theological level, he perceives a downward shift of the functions—Odhin has become primarily a battle-god, Thor has become more a god of farmers than of warriors, and the Vanir have been "pushed" into a rather limited sphere concerned with matters such as "human fecundity and voluptuousness" (123).

Dumézil overlooks, however, that shifts "upward" occurred as well. The free farmers, whom Dumézil tends to dismiss as "peasants," were also warriors in Germanic society. Though some distinction between ordinary men and the aristocracy existed, the great social divide in Germanic culture was between the free and the unfree, and free men were armed men. As Green says, "The right to bear arms and to play a part in the tribal assembly was also a duty: both were the prerogative of freemen in Germanic society" (39). He further notes that words such as *heri* and *folk* referred equally to "the people" and "the army" (90) until Roman and then Christian influence caused a "demotion of the freeman" as the king asserted ever-increasing authority (99-100). Thus, among the Germanic peoples, free men and the gods they worship are warriors by definition, and the Second Function has expanded to include everyone except slaves (who were never part of the tripartite social structure to begin with). Frey, too, is a warrior as a matter of course, and he will fight alongside Odhin and Thor at Ragnarok.

In addition, Frey has acquired a number of First Function characteristics. First, some background: Dumézil defines the First Function as including both "magic and juridical sovereignty" (*Gods* 118). In India, these two components of sovereignty are represented by the two gods Varuna and Mitra, respectively (*Mitra-Varuna* 72):

> Mitra is the sovereign under his reasoning aspect, luminous, ordered, calm, benevolent, priestly; Varuna is the sovereign under his attacking aspect, dark, inspired, violent, terrible, warlike.

Dumézil makes a convincing case, first, that this dual concept of sovereignty is indigenous to Indo-European culture, and, second, that the Germanic gods Odhin and Tyr descend from this ancestral pattern.

Dumézil also notes, however, that Tyr "is visibly at the end of a long retreat by the time of our documents" (*Gods* 35). I contend that some of the characteristics associated with the "Mitra" pattern were assimilated by Frey, especially in places like Sweden where Tyr never seems to have held much importance. The clearest evidence for this lies in a comparison of Frey with the leaders and priests of Rome. Dumézil notes that Romulus and Numa, Rome's first rulers, form a pair of the Varuna/Mitra type. Romulus is a warrior and "terrible sovereign." In contrast, Numa's reign recalls Frey's and Frodhi's: "peace remains unbroken" and internal stability is maintained under Numa (*Mitra-Varuna* 51). Like Frey, Numa is connected with oaths (55). Numa "established an annual sacrifice to Fides" (55); similarly, Frø [=Frey] "altered the ancient system of sacrifice... by instituting the slaughter of human victims[1]" at Uppsala (Saxo I.73). Numa also establishes a new class of priest, the *flamen dialis*. Like the brahmans of India, whom Dumézil identifies with Mitra (*Mitra-Varuna* 73), "their role is essentially to provide stable prosperity and regular fecundity" (25), and "flamines and brahmans are the guardians of sacred order" (34). Both these groups of priests are subject to extensive prohibitions. In the

---

[1] Fisher's translation.

Germanic world, there is far less distinction between priests and other men, but the few prohibitions that do exist—the bans on carrying weapons and riding stallions, plus the fact that Frey instituted mound-burial in place of cremation—recall (albeit in less extreme form) some of those Dumézil lists (24):

> The flamen dialis must not so much as look upon armed troops...; the brahman must suspend his sacred knowledge...whenever he hears the hiss of arrows, or is in the midst of an army, and so on.
>
> The flamen dialis...must neither mount a horse...nor, even for the purpose of sacrifice, touch one...; the brahman must not study on horseback nor, it seems, sit on any animal or in any vehicle.
>
> The flamen dialis must not approach a funeral pyre...; the brahman must avoid the smoke from a funeral pyre and must cease his sacred studies in any village where a funeral procession is passing.

Finally, whereas Varuna is a god of binding, "[t]he flamen dialis is an 'unbinder': any man in chains who takes refuge with him is immediately set free" (95). In *Lokasenna*, Tyr(!) says of Frey that he *leysir ór höptom hvern*, "releases everyone from fetters" (37.4). In some ways, Frey does not fit the "Mitra" pattern—most noticeably, he shows much more vigor and vitality than is typical for the sober, earnest types described above—but nonetheless I think it is fair to see in Frey an example of the "pious, peace-loving kings" that Dumézil places squarely within his First Function (90).

Thus, Frey combines in himself the First Function attributes of a priest-king and the Second Function abilities of a warrior while maintaining his Third Function power to grant good harvests and prosperity. Yet this very combination of all three Functions again associates him with sovereignty in Dumézil's system: "the 'function of sovereignty' is the only one that potentially contains all the others and can easily actualize these potentialities" (*Gods* 36).

A final comment on the concept of "sovereignty": to understand Frey, what matters in the end is, not Dumézil's nor anyone else's analysis of the abstract concept, but rather what the members of Germanic society themselves believed and expected (insofar as we can determine it from the surviving evidence). If we could ask a 10th-century Swede about the "function" of his king, he might well reply: to protect holy places and make the sacrifices that ensure *ár*. To uphold the law and defend the land to preserve *friðr*. In short, to be like Yngvi-Frey.

Poetic Texts
and Translations

This Appendix describes the poems quoted in this work. Though various translations were consulted, the translations that appear in this work (and any errors therein) are my own.

Eddic Poems: The majority of the poems cited come from the collection generally known as the *Poetic Edda*. Various editors differ regarding which poems should properly be considered "Eddic"; I have followed Larrington's selection. Verse and line numbers used in this work are based on her edition. Table B1 lists the Eddic poems cited in this work, their corresponding titles and page numbers in Larrington's translation, and on-line sources for the Old Norse text. I also consulted translations of the *Poetic Edda* by Bellows, Bray, Dronke, Hollander, and Terry; for *Völuspá*, *Lokasenna* and *Skírnismál*, Dronke's detailed commentary was especially valuable. Finally, Faulkes' translation of Snorri's *Edda* contains an excellent translation of *Gróttasöngr*.

Other poems: For *Beowulf*, Chickering's edition provides an excellent translation with facing-page Old English text; line numbers in this work refer to his edition. Halsall's edition of the Old English *Rune Poem* gives the original text and her translations for that poem (86-93) as well as for the

Norwegian and Icelandic *Rune Poems* (181-6); Dickins' older edition also contains the original text and his translations of all three *Rune Poems*. Finally, an English translation of Einar Helgason's *Vellekla* is given in Hollander's *Skalds*. For the Old Norse text, Snorri's *Haraldar saga gráfeldar* and *Ólafs saga Tryggvasonar* include several verses. Verse 18, which the sagas omit, is given in Gade (17).

Table B1. Texts from the *Poetic Edda*.

English titles and page numbers are from
Larrington's translation.

Norse title	English title	pp.
Grímnismál	"Grimnir's Sayings"	50-60
Gróttasöngr	"Song of Grotti"	260-263
Guðrúnarkviða II	"Second Lay of Gudrun"	196-202
Hávamál	"Sayings of the High One"	14-38
Helgakviða Hjörvarðssonar	"The Poem of Helgi Hiorvardsson"	123-131
Hyndluljóð	"The Song of Hyndla"	253-259
Lokasenna	"Loki's Quarrel"	84-96
Skírnismál	"Skirnir's Journey"	61-68
Vafþrúðnismál	"Vafthrudnir's Sayings"	39-49
Völuspá	"The Seeress's Prophecy"	3-13

Bibliography

Primary Sources

Note: "ON" = Old Norse. For works in Old Norse, both original texts and English translations are listed. References in this work are to chapter numbers in the ON sources; these usually, but not always, correspond to the chapter numbers in the English translations listed below. Exceptions to the practice of citing ON chapter numbers are *The Saga of King Heidrek the Wise* and *Flateyjarbók*, for which page numbers are given.

Adam of Bremen. *History of the Archbishops of Hamburg-Bremen.* Trans. Francis J. Tschan. New York: Columbia UP, 2002.

Bede, *Ecclesiastical History of the English People.* Revised ed. Trans. Leo Sherley-Price. London: Penguin, 1990.

Beowulf. Trans. Howell D. Chickering, Jr. New York: Anchor, 1977. [See also Appendix B.]

The Book of Settlements: Landnámabók. Trans. Hermann Pálsson and Paul Edwards. Manitoba: U Manitoba P, 1972. [ON: *Landnámabók.*]

Brandkrossa þáttur. Netútgáfan Fornrit Íslendingaþættir <http://www.snerpa.is/net/isl/brandk.htm>. Accessed 12 July 2007. [English translation: "Brandkrossi's Tale."]

"Brandkrossi's Tale." Hreinsson 4: 442-6. Trans. John Porter. [ON: *Brandkrossa þáttur.*]

Brennu-Njáls saga. Netútgáfan Fornrit Íslendingasögur <http://www.snerpa.is/net/isl/njala.htm>. Accessed 12 July 2007. [English translation: "Njal's Saga."]

Dickins, Bruce. *Runic and Heroic Poems of the Old Teutonic Peoples.* Cambridge: Cambridge UP, 1915. [See also Appendix B.]

Egils saga. Netútgáfan Fornrit Íslendingasögur <http://www.snerpa.is/net/isl/egils.htm>. Accessed July 12 2007. [English translation: "Egil's Saga."]

"Egil's Saga." Hreinnson 1: 33-177. Trans. Bernard Scudder. [ON: *Egils saga.*]

Einar Helgason (*skálaglamm*). *Vellekla*: see Appendix B.

Eyrbyggja saga. Netútgáfan Fornrit Íslendingasögur <http://www.snerpa.is/net/isl/eyrbygg.htm>. Accessed 12 July 2007. [English translation: "The Saga of the People of Eyri."]

Flateyjarbók. 3 vols. Ed.Guðbrandr Vifusson and C.R. Unger. Christiania: P.T. Malling, 1860-1868.

Gísla saga Súrssonar. Netútgáfan Fornrit Íslendingasögur <http://www.snerpa.is/net/isl/gisl.htm>. Accessed 12 July 2007. [English translation: "Gisli Sursson's Saga."]

"Gisli Sursson's Saga." Hreinsson 2: 1-48. Trans. Martin S. Regal. [ON: *Gísla saga Súrssonar.*]

Grímnismál. Netútgáfan Fornrit Kvæði Fornkvæði <http://www.snerpa.is/net/kvaedi/grimnir.htm>. Accessed 13 July 2007. [English translation: see Appendix B.]

Gróttasöngr. Norrænir textar og kvæði: Eddukvæði <http://www.heimskringla.no/original/edda/grottasongr. php>. Accessed 13 July 2007. [English translation: see Appendix B.]

Guðrúnarkviða II (*"in forna"*). Norrænir textar og kvæði: Eddukvæði <http://www.heimskringla.no/original/edda/gudrunarkvi

dainforna.php>. Accessed 13 July 2007. [English translation: see Appendix B.]

Hallfreðar saga vandræðaskálds (eftir Möðruvallabók). Netútgáfan Fornrit Íslendingasögur <http://www.snerpa.is/net/isl/hallf.htm>. Accessed July 12 2007. [English translation: "The Saga of Hallfred the Troublesome Poet."]

Halsall, Maureen. *The Old English* Rune Poem: *A Critical Edition.* Toronto: U Toronto P, 1981. [See also Appendix B.]

Hávamál. Netútgáfan Fornrit Kvæði Fornkvæði <http://www.snerpa.is/net/kvaedi/havamal.htm>. Accessed 13 July 2007. [English translation: see Appendix B.]

Helgakviða Hjörvarðssonar. Norrænir textar og kvæði: Eddukvæði <http://www.heimskringla.no/original/edda/helgakvidah jorvardssonar.php>. Accessed 13 July 2007. [English translation: see Appendix B.]

Hollander, Lee M. *The Skalds: A Selection of Their Poems, With Introductions and Notes.* Princeton: Princeton UP 1945.

Hrafnkels saga Freysgoða. Netútgáfan Fornrit Íslendingasögur <http://www.snerpa.is/net/isl/hrafn.htm>. Accessed 12 July 2007. [English translation: "The Saga of Hrafnkel Frey's Godi."]

Hreinsson, Viðar, ed. *Complete Sagas of Icelanders.* 5 vols. Reykjavík: Leifur Eiríksson, 1997.

Hyndluljóð. Norrænir textar og kvæði: Eddukvæði <http://www.heimskringla.no/original/edda/hyndluljod.p hp>. Accessed 13 July 2007. [English translation: see Appendix B.]

"Killer-Glum's Saga." Hreinsson 2: 267-314. Trans. John McKinnell. [ON: *Víga-Glúms saga.*]

Kormáks saga. Netútgáfan Fornrit Íslendingasögur
<http://www.snerpa.is/net/isl/kormaks.htm>. Accessed
12 July 2007. [English translation: "Kormak's Saga."]
"Kormak's Saga." Hreinsson 1: 179-224. Trans. Rory
McTurk. [ON: *Kormáks saga.*]
Landnámabók (Sturlubók). Netútgáfan Fornrit
<http://www.snerpa.is/net/snorri/landnama.htm>.
Accessed 12 July 2007. [English translation: *The Book
of Settlements.*]
Lokasenna. Netútgáfan Fornrit Kvæði Fornkvæði
<http://www.snerpa.is/net/kvaedi/lokasenn.htm>.
Accessed 13 July 2007. [English translation: see
Appendix B.]
"Njal's Saga." Hreinsson 3: 1-220. Trans. Robert Cook.
[ON: *Brennu-Njáls saga.*]
Ögmundar þáttur dytts. Netútgáfan Fornrit Íslendingaþættir
<http://www.snerpa.is/net/isl/dytts.htm>. Accessed 12
July 2007. [English translation: "The Tale of Ogmund
Bash."]
The Poetic Edda. All translations mentioned in Appendix B
are listed here by translator:
Bellows, Henry Adams, trans. *The Poetic Edda.*
Lewiston, NY: Edwin Mellon, 1991. [Reprint of the
original.]
Bray, Olive, trans. *The Elder or Poetic Edda. Part I. The
Mythological Poems.* New York: AMS, 1982.
[Reprint of the 1908 edition.]
Dronke, Ursula, ed., trans. *The Poetic Edda: Volume II.
Mythological Poems.* Oxford: Clarendon, 1997.
Hollander, Lee M., trans. *The Poetic Edda.* Austin: U
Texas P, 1962.
Larrington, Carolyne, trans. *The Poetic Edda.* Oxford:
Oxford UP, 1996.
Terry, Patricia, trans. *Poems of the Elder Edda: Revised
Edition.* Philadelphia: U Pennsylvania P, 1990.

"The Saga of Hallfred the Troublesome Poet." Hreinsson 1: 225-53. Trans. Diana Whaley. [ON: *Hallfreðar saga vandræðaskálds.*]

The Saga of King Heidrek the Wise. Ed. Christopher Tolkien. Edinburgh: Thomas Nelson, 1960. [This edition contains both the Old Norse text and an English translation; see also "The Saga of Hervör and Heithrek."]

"The Saga of Hervör and Heithrek." *Stories and Ballads of the Far Past.* Trans. N. Kershaw. Cambridge: Cambridge UP 1921. [ON: <http://www.home.ix.netcom.com/%7Ekyamazak/myth/norse/kershaw/NLS-hervor-is.htm>. Accessed 26 July 2007.]

"The Saga of Hrafnkel Frey's Godi." Hreinsson 5: 291-81. Trans. Terry Gunnell. [ON: *Hrafnkels saga Freysgoða.*]

"The Saga of the People of Eyri." Hreinsson 5: 131-218. Trans. Judy Quinn. [ON: *Eyrbyggja saga.*]

"The Saga of the People of Vatnsdal." Hreinsson 4: 1-66. Trans. Andrew Wawn. [ON: *Vatnsdæla saga.*]

The Saga of the Volsungs: the Norse Epic of Sigurd the Dragon Slayer. Trans. Jesse L. Byock. Berkeley: U California P, 1990. [ON: *Völsunga saga*].

Saxo Grammaticus. *The History of the Danes, Books I-IX.* Ed. Hilda Ellis Davidson. Trans. Peter Fisher. Woodbridge, Suffolk: D.S. Brewer, 1980.

Skírnismál. Netútgáfan Fornrit Kvæði Fornkvæði <http://www.snerpa.is/net/kvaedi/skirnir.htm>. Accessed 13 July 2007. [English translation: see Appendix B.]

Snorri Sturluson. *Edda.* Trans. Anthony Faulkes. London: J.M. Dent & Sons, 1987. [ON: *Gylfaginning*; *Skáldskaparmál*; *Þulur*]

– – –. *Gylfaginning.* Norrænir textar og kvæði: Edda Snorra Sturlusonar <http://www.heimskringla.no/original/snorre/gylfaginni

ng.php>. Accessed 12 July 2007 [English translation: *Edda* 7-58.]

– – –. *Hákonar saga Aðalsteinsfóstra.* Netútgáfan Fornrit Heimskringla <http://www.snerpa.is/net/snorri/hakong.htm>. Accessed 13 July 2007. [English translation: *Heimskringla* 77-101 ("Hacon the Good").]

– – –. *Hálfdanar saga svarta.* Netútgáfan Fornrit Heimskringla <http://www.snerpa.is/net/snorri/halfdsv.htm>. Accessed 13 July 2007. [English translation: *Heimskringla* 36-42 ("Halvdan the Black").]

– – –. *Haraldar saga gráfeldar.* Netútgáfan Fornrit Heimskringla <http://www.snerpa.is/net/snorri/hgrafel.htm>. Accessed 13 July 2007. [English translation: *Heimskringla* 102-114 ("Eric's Sons" and "Hacon the Jarl").]

– – –. *Heimskringla, or The Lives of the Norse Kings.* Ed. Erling Monsen. Trans. Erling Monsen and A.H. Smith. New York: Dover, 1990.

– – –. *Heimskringla Prologus.* Netútgáfan Fornrit Heimskringla <http://www.snerpa.is/net/snorri/prolog.htm>. Accessed 13 July 2007. [English translation: *Heimskringla* xxxv-xxxvii ("Preface").]

– – –. *Ólafs saga Tryggvasonar.* Netútgáfan Fornrit Heimskringla <http://www.snerpa.is/net/snorri/oltr.htm>. Accessed 13 July 2007. [English translation: *Heimskringla* 115-217 ("Olav Trygvason").]

– – –. *Skáldskaparmál.* Norrænir textar og kvæði: Edda Snorra Sturlusonar <http://www.heimskringla.no/original/snorre/skaldskapa rmal.php>. Accessed 12 July 2007. [English translation: *Edda* 59-155.]

– – –. *Þulur.* Norrænir textar og kvæði: Edda Snorra Sturlusonar <http://www.heimskringla.no/original/snorre/nafnathulu

r.php>. Accessed 12 July 2007. [English translation: *Edda* 155-164.]

– – –. *Ynglinga saga*. Netútgáfan Fornrit Heimskringla <http://www.snerpa.is/net/snorri/yngl-sag.htm>. Accessed 13 July 2007. [English translation: *Heimskringla* 1-35.]

"Sorli's Story." *Six Old Icelandic Sagas*. Trans. W. Bryant Bachman, Jr. and Guðmundur Erlingsson. Lanham, MD: UP America, 1993. [ON: *Sörla þáttur.*]

Sörla þáttur eða Héðins saga ok Högna. Netútgáfan Fornrit Fornaldarsögur Norðurlanda <http://www.snerpa.is/net/forn/sorla.htm>. Accessed 14 July 2007. [English translation: "Sorli's Story."]

Tacitus. *Germania*. Trans. J.B. Rives. Oxford: Clarendon, 1999.

"The Tale of Ogmund Bash." Hreinson 2: 314-22. Trans. John McKinnell. [ON: *Ögmundar þáttur dytts.*]

Vafþrúðnismál. Netútgáfan Fornrit Kvæði Fornkvæði <http://www.snerpa.is/net/kvaedi/vafthrud.htm>. Accessed 13 July 2007. [English translation: see Appendix B.]

Vatnsdæla saga. Netútgáfan Fornrit Íslendingasögur <http://www.snerpa.is/net/isl/vatnsdae.htm>. Accessed 12 July 2007. [English translation: "The Saga of the People of Vatnsdal."]

Víga-Glúms saga. Netútgáfan Fornrit Íslendingasögur <http://www.snerpa.is/net/isl/vigaglum.htm>. Accessed 12 July 2007. [English translation: "Killer-Glum's Saga."]

Völsunga saga. Netútgáfan Fornrit Fornaldarsögur Norðurlanda <http://www.snerpa.is/net/forn/volsung.htm>. Accessed 12 July 2007. [English translation: *The Saga of the Volsungs.*]

Völuspá. Netútgáfan Fornrit Kvæði Fornkvæði <http://www.snerpa.is/net/kvaedi/volospa.htm>.

Accessed 13 July 2007. [English translation: see Appendix B.]

Secondary Sources

Baetke, Walter. *Das Heilige im Germanischen*. Tübingen: J.C.B. Mohr, 1942.

Bosworth, Joseph. *An Anglo-Saxon Dictionary*. Ed. N. Northcote Toller. Oxford: Oxford UP, 1898.

Byock, Jesse L. *Medieval Iceland: Society, Sagas, and Power*. Berkeley: U California P, 1988.

Cleasby, Richard and Gudbrand Vigfusson. *An Icelandic-English Dictionary*. 2nd ed. Oxford: Oxford UP, 1957.

Dronke, Ursula. *Skírnismál*: Commentary on the Text. *The Poetic Edda: Volume II. Mythological Poems*. Trans. Ursula Dronke. Oxford: Clarendon, 1997. 404-14.

Dumézil, Georges. *Archaic Roman Religion*. Vol 1. Trans. Philip Krapp. Chicago: U Chicago P, 1970. 2 vols. [Translation of *La Religion archaïque*, 1966.]

– – –. *Gods of the Ancient Northmen*. Ed. Einar Haugen. Berkeley: U California P, 1973. [Translation of *Les Dieux des Germains*, 1959.]

– – –. *Mitra-Varuna: An Essay on Two Indo-European Representations of Sovereignty*. Trans. Derek Coltman. New York: Zone, 1988. [Dumézil's original essay is dated 1947.]

Ellis, Hilda Roderick. *The Road to Hel: A Study of the Conception of the Dead in Old Norse Literature*. New York: Greenwood, 1968.

Ellis Davidson, Hilda. Book Five: Introduction. *The History of the Danes*. By Saxo Grammaticus. Ed. Hilda Ellis Davidson. Trans. Peter Fisher. Woodbridge, Suffolk: D.S. Brewer, 1980. I.113-7.

– – –. Commentary on the Text. *The History of the Danes*.

By Saxo Grammaticus. Ed. Hilda Ellis Davidson. Trans. Peter Fisher. Woodbridge, Suffolk: D.S. Brewer, 1980. II.17-165,

– – – . "Milk and the Northern Goddess." *The Concept of the Goddess*. Ed. Sandra Billington and Miranda Green. New York: Routledge, 1996. 91-106.

Ellis Davidson, H.R. *Myths and Symbols in Pagan Europe: Early Scandinavian and Celtic Religions*. Syracuse, NY: Syracuse UP, 1988.

Elves, Trolls and Elemental Beings. Trans. Alan Boucher. Icelandic Folktales II. Reykjavik: Iceland Review, 1977.

Foote, Peter and David M. Wilson. *The Viking Achievement: the Society and Culture of Early Medieval Scandinavia*. London: Sidgwick and Jackson, 1970.

Gade, Kari Ellen. *The Structure of Old Norse* Dróttkvætt *Poetry*. Islandica 49. Ithaca: Cornell UP, 1995.

Green, D.H. *Language and History in the Early Germanic World*. Cambridge: Cambridge UP, 1998.

Halsall, Maureen. Explanatory Notes. *The Old English* Rune Poem*: A Critical Edition*. Ed. Maureen Halsall. Toronto: U Toronto P, 1981. 95-163.

Lindow, John. *Norse Mythology: A Guide to the Gods, Heroes, Rituals, and Beliefs*. Oxford: Oxford UP, 2001.

North, Richard. *Heathen Gods in Old English Literature*. Cambridge Studies in Anglo-Saxon England 22. Cambridge: Cambridge UP, 1997.

Orchard, Andy. *Dictionary of Norse Myth and Legend*. London: Cassell, 1998.

Rives, R.B. Commentary. *Germania*. By Tacitus. Oxford: Clarendon, 1999. 99-328.

Simek, Rudolf. *Dictionary of Northern Mythology*. Trans. Angela Hall. Woodbridge, Suffolk: D.S. Brewer, 1993.

Turville-Petre, E.O.G. *Myth and Religion of the North: The Religion of Ancient Scandinavia*. Westport, CT: Greenwood, 1975. [Reprint of 1964 edition.]

Watkins, Calvert. *The American Heritage Dictionary of Indo-European Roots*. 2nd ed. Boston: Houghton Mifflin, 2000.

Index

www.ingramcontent.com/pod-product-compliance
Lightning Source LLC
Chambersburg PA
CBHW031258280526
45784CB00004B/1898